POSTWAR SPORTS CARS
THE MODERN CLASSICS

ERIC DYMOCK

POSTWAR SPORTS CARS
THE MODERN CLASSICS

a Charles Herridge book

Acknowledgements

© Copyright Charles Herridge Ltd

First published in Great Britain in 1981 by Ebury Press

This edition published in 1984 by Charles Herridge Ltd, Woodacott, Northam, Bideford, Devon EX39 1NB

ISBN 0 946569 06 1

Printed in Yugoslavia

AC Cars: 38 bottom
Alfa Romeo (GB)' 40 both, 41
Alvis Ltd.: 27 bottom
Aston Martin Lagonda: 42, 43 both, 46, 149
Autocar: 12, 13, 14, 17, 24, 26, 27 top, 28 both,
    29, 32, 36 44, 45 top, 48/49, 52, 53, 54, 56,
    58/59, 63, 65 both, 68 both, 81 three, 86, 88,
    93, 97, 100, 102/3, 104/5, 107 top, 112, 115,
    116, 123, 124, 125, 126, 139, 140, 142,
    143 both, 144, 145, 147 top, 148, 158, 162/3,
    172, 176, 177, 178/9, 185.
Automobile Monteverdi: 153
Bertone: 73 bottom, 129 bottom
BL: 10, 18, 31, 95 both, 141, 160, 164 bottom,
    165 top, 166
BL Heritage: 92, 94, 180/1, 183
BMW (GB): 47, 50
Citroen: 16, 170/1
Datsun (GB): 173
Delorean: 174/5, 175
Eric Dymock: 25, 45 bottom, 71, 96, 98,
    147 bottom
Fiat: 127
Fiat (GB): 77 both, 78/9, 130/1
Ford Motor Co.: 132/3, 134/5, 137, 138
Ford Motor Co. Lincoln Cars: 136
General Motors: 118/9 both, 120 both, 182
W. K. Henderson: 140 bottom
Jaguar Cars: 10, 66/7, 69 both, 70
Jensen Motors: 145, 146
Lamborghini: 72, 73 top
Lancia: 75, 76 both
Lotus Cars: 30 top, 80, 83 both, 84/5
Jem Marsh: 150
Matra: 152 top and bottom
Mercedes-Benz (GB): 30 bottom, 90 both, 91
Motor: 11, 37, 38 both, 82
George Oliver: 20
Peugeot: 110, 111
Pininfarina: 34/5, 55 both, 57 both, 60,
    61 both, 113 both, 121, 122, 128, 129 top
Pininfarina (GB): 39 right
Porsche (GB): 33, 107 bottom, 108, 109 both
Reliant Motor Co.: 154
Renault (GB): 155, 156 both
Rootes: 26, 157 both
Saab (GB): 184
Shell: 101
Standard-Triumph: 161 both, 164 both,
    165 bottom
Talbot: 151, 152 middle
Talbot PSA: 34 bottom, 159
TVR: 167
VAG: 169
Vauxhall Motors: 168 both

CONTENTS

PREFACE

Rather than decide what a sports car is, it may be easier to decide what it is not. Then, by a process of elimination, we can be left with some idea of what we are talking about. I know what a sports car is, and so probably do you, but there is the rest of the world to think of, and they must be left in no doubt.

First, a sports car is never dull. That rules out any number of worthy vehicles mass-produced to transport the millions on their daily comings and goings. Second, sports cars are never slow. That is not the same as saying they are always fast. Moreover many sports cars which were fast in their day have been over-taken by time and technical development. Third, sports cars *may* not be roomy. A car designed with perform-ance in mind is likely to make concessions to luxury for the sake of weight-saving or streamlining. Fourth, sports cars generally have some connections with motoring sport. It may be a close relationship with racing, as in the case of Ferrari, or it may be a line of descent from trials and rally cars such as the Morgan. Both are indisputably sports cars, yet they are as unlike as cars can be: both, in their ways, market leaders, cherished by their owners, appreciating assets, and included amongst the great classics.

On the other hand, they may have no connection with sport at all. Lambor-ghini were careful not to get involved with racing, yet their cars had all the best characteristics of the race-bred Ferraris, also built in one of the great homes of the sporting motor car, the Plain of Lombardy.

Not all sports cars were or are extravagantly expensive. MG and Austin-Healey made cars that were sporting by any definition, based on components as mundane as those of the Austin A35 and the Morris Minor. They

were never what one might call excl-usive either, being turned out by the hundred thousand, unlike the rich, bespoke 'one-offs' made at fancy prices elsewhere.

There is no commonality of style or capacity. Sports cars have been large and small, open and closed, front-engined, mid-engined, and rear-eng-ined, yet almost *never* front wheel drive. The inherent characteristic of under-steer, with all that means in making a car feel out-of-balance, stretches the definition to cover front-drive cars in only a very few exceptional cases, such as the Mini-Cooper — a car capable of winning the Monte Carlo Rally can hardly escape being called a sports car.

There are other things sports cars are not. For example, since about 1960 they have not been — for our purposes at any rate — the same as sports-racing cars. This represents a convenient watershed, when racing regulations encouraged the design of cars which must be regarded as two-seat racing cars rather than sports cars in the tradition of Le

Developed by the BMC works team, the big Austin-Healey became a formidable rally car. Despite the problems of cockpit overheating and low ground clearance which plagued production cars, it scored some spectacular successes in long-distance events such as the Liège-Sofia-Liège. Timo Makinen is seen here on the Craigvinean special stage in Scotland during the RAC Rally, in which victory always eluded the powerful, spectacular and handsome car.

opposite
The essence of sports car motoring. A Jaguar E-Type drives past the pits on the old Rheims Grand Prix circuit, long since overgrown and disused.

Cement dust laid to soak up spilled oil at Le Mans is raised by the Porsche 907 of Spoerry/Steinemann (66) which finished second in the 1968 24 Hours classic, and the Chevrolet Corvette Sting Ray of Maglioli/Greder, which retired with engine trouble after 5 hours' racing.

Mans classics such as the D-Type Jaguar or the Talbot Lago. Thereafter they would, with a few honourable exceptions such as the GT 40, develop into cars generally unsuitable for use on the road. And a sports car is not the same thing as a racing car.

A sports car is not exactly the same as a GT car either, although in some cases it might be. The reason for equivocation is that all Ferraris must be considered sports cars, yet some are, by definition Grand Touring. The title was surely coined to describe cars suitable for taking the Grand Tour, that educational experience beloved of the Victorians which took in the architectural gems and fashionable watering places of the Low Countries, the Alps, Apennines, and Classical Greece. Such a car would need some, at least, of the attributes of a sports car, so in many cases the distinction must be blurred.

Sports cars in the postwar world went through some painful metamorphoses. The birth pangs of those which saw the light of day between 1945 and 1960 were severe, at a time when the traditional conception of a sports car changed with a totality which seemed to spell the

end of the category altogether. They were threatened by technical developments, then political and economic influences looked like prohibiting the very idea of anything so frivolous as a car made for any purpose beyond mere transportation.

Cars that were faster than strictly necessary became socially suspect. In many places they were all but outlawed — in most countries they remained abhorrent to the bureaucrat, obscene to the narrow-minded ecologist, and almost blasphemous to churchmen. Cars using extra energy for the sake of speed were made to appear selfish and unnecessary. Safety campaigners blamed them for ills as diverse as petty crime and displays of virility; above all as symbols for the glorification of speed. Detractors denounced them as sexist and socially divisive.

It was surprising that sports cars survived at all, but they did. No longer perhaps the racy two-seater with the rag top of yore, demand nonetheless persisted for a car with a better turn of speed, a car which worked better, or a car that was simply different from the general run of the (motor) mills of

Europe, the United States, and Japan.

Discriminating clients continued to demand the one-off, expensive sporting classic. Sufficient enthusiasts remained to support the ready-to-race-or-rally stripped-down coupe or saloon. Some of the interest was whipped-up, to be sure, by car manufacturers' skilful marketing and support for racing. Yet it was not regarded as cynical to apply knowledge gained in the course of a competition programme to the benefit of mass transportation of the millions. And racing, or at least the forcing-house and incentive that racing provides, *did* benefit the mass market. As far as marketing and advertising was concerned, it proved more profitable to take the hitherto down-market two-door model, call it a sports coupe (or merely imply the term — insurance companies came to regard 'sports' with the deepest apprehension) and mark it up at a premium price. These cut-and-shut models sometimes outran the customary sports car, and when they did, enthusiasts drove them in their thousands, with the racy thoroughbred sometimes very hard-pressed to keep up.

Despite analysts' analogies which put the motor car in the same consumer category as the washing machine and the domestic refrigerator, it refused to remain there. It steadfastly maintained the sort of appeal once exercised by horses, gratifying urges as primitive as merely showing off, and as explicit as snobbery. It was precisely this adoption of the motor car as a means of recreation that gave it the significance of a good hunter, or a well-rigged yacht. The sports car ranked with the gun and the rod, the Purdey (or Holland and Holland if you must) and the Hardy; the sporting implement where the craft virtues of balance, style, quality, efficiency and accuracy complemented the sportsman's skill, dexterity, or even daring. Yet, as with bat, racquet, club, or ball, what mattered most was performance. You could have elegance, proportion, expense and reputation, but without performance you had nothing.

Consequently, we need no longer be concerned with deciding exactly what a sports car is. As a term it was invented, according to the eminent G. N. Georgano, by *The Autocar* in February 1919 in an article which used the terms 'sports car' or 'sporting car' for the first time and at length, although the basis of the type was laid down early in the century as something between a racing car and a touring car — both easily definable. A

specific instance in 1903 is sometimes taken as the establishment of the category, when fire destroyed the three special 90 hp Mercedes cars built for the Gordon Bennett race by the factory at Canstatt.

With much at stake, Mercedes had to scour the Continent for substitutes, and were forced to enter three 60 hp cars, one from their American customer Clarence Dinsmore, and two from their Paris distributor. In the event, the 60 proved a better bet, and although two retired, the fierce, red-bearded Belgian Camille Jenatzy won in an uncharacteristically steady drive. To convert the cars for racing, Mercedes merely removed their five-seat tonneau bodies, lamps, mudguards, and other heavy gear, and mounted lightweight seats for driver and mechanic, together with lightweight wings. Moreover, the cars were driven from Germany to Ireland, where the race took place, and back again afterwards.

This Mercedes was probably the best-handling production car of the time, and also one of the fastest, with a top speed of over 60 mph even with its touring body. It finds its place in history

The efficiency and exemplary handling of Porsches made them popular rally cars. Here a competitor tackles an Alpine Rally in an open Porsche which, known as the Speedster with 1.5 litre and later 1.6 litre engines, became a popular 'clubman' racer in the United States.

of course as the founder of the racing connection which, by definition, associates sports cars with sport. Motoring sport is not the same as motor racing however, and many sports cars to come were developed for rallies and trials instead.

A great deal has been made of the role played by the Prince Henry Trials in the development of the sports car. Grand Prix racing was developing from the Gordon Bennett series of contests, the Automobile Club de France initiating their 'Great Prize' event for out-and-out racing cars in 1906. But individuals were left with nothing in which to enter their touring cars. In 1905 the Automobile Club of Great Britain and Ireland (later the RAC) organized the first Tourist Trophy race on the Isle of Man, won by J. S. Napier in his Scottish Arrol-Johnston. Captain Percy Northey was second, in a Rolls-Royce 20 which was to win the following year in the hands of the Hon. C. S. Rolls. Meanwhile, the example of the TT had been followed elsewhere.

The scope of competition for touring cars was expanded by a contest established under the sponsorship of the portraitist Professor Hubert von Herkomer RA. He instituted the International Touring Competition for the Herkomer Trophy, consisting of a road section, a hill-climb, and a speed trial, thus effectively inventing what came to be known as the rally. The object of the affair was not to determine which touring car was necessarily the fastest — that was the concern of out-and-out racing. But in a commendable effort to 'improve the breed', Professor Herkomer was trying to establish which was the most reliable, a more important consideration for a touring car, after all, at a time when many of them were hopelessly prone to breakdowns. Thus, at this early stage, reliability became an important feature of sports car racing, whereas in Grand Prix racing speed was to remain the very essence.

The importance of the Herkomer Trials lay in their pioneering role, foreshadowing and leading to the rather more famous Prince Henry Trials. Prince Heinrich of Prussia, younger brother of the Kaiser, was a keen driver. It should be remembered, incidentally, that motoring was not primarily a driving activity, even amongst people who regarded themselves as keen motorists. Motoring as a pastime consisted of being taken for a ride in a motor car rather as one might take a ride in a carriage or a railway

left
The relationship between sports cars and racing cars was exemplified best by Ferrari. The Dino engine — in effect a whole family of V-6 engines — was used to power Formula 1 Ferraris and an entire generation of road cars. Here it is in four-cam 1960 form in the last front-engined Ferrari Grand Prix car. The red crackle finish on the cam covers was characteristic of the Bugatti school of engineering, which demanded good looks as well as good performance.

The singular lines of the Citroen SM were as original as its engineering. The first pictures, released on 11 March, 1970, revealed a car of great distinction, utterly unlike any sports or Grand Touring car ever made.

train. Mastering the technicalities and the controls was a matter for the adventurous, the skilled, and the expert.

Prince Heinrich was sufficiently expert to compete in the Herkomer, and a few months after the last of them, in 1907, announced he would present a trophy for a similar competition, starting in Berlin on 7 June 1908.

Despite regulations intended to encourage amateur sportsmen, results were important for sales, and factory-supported teams designed cars which advanced the art and science of the touring car much faster than hitherto. Once again a principle was established. Motoring sport provided an incentive to make a more efficient car, and the rigours of competition would show whether it worked. The rules — as the rules for motoring competition ever would — only taxed the ingenuity of engineers in devising ways of getting round them.

The Horch team turned up with four-seat bodies in which the space between the front and rear passengers was cowled-in to provide better stream-lining. They had no doors, and deeply flared wings. They also had neither hood nor windscreen, marking yet another characteristic of the sports car — the sacrifices occupants had to make for the sake of speed.

Yet the Prince Henry Trials contri-buted more than a set of design criteria

for the sports car. One of the drivers in the first event was a still little-known member of a family of sculptors and artists, Ettore Bugatti. In the 1910 event an Austro-Daimler appeared, designed by the young Ferdinand Porsche. This event also began the fashion for nam-ing sports cars after the competitions. Although less successful than the Aus-tro-Daimler, two of the 3 litre Vauxhall team managed non-stop runs, and with elegant Vee radiators, low build, and a flexible top gear performance, came to be called 'Prince Henry' Vauxhalls. They were also developed with a larger, more powerful engine into a famous series of sports cars culminating in the postwar 30/98.

Thus were the traditions, character, and philosophy of the sporting car created. They became fashionable and chic, whether they were used for sport or not. Demand for them came from men such as the young Prince Henry, who discovered satisfaction in handling a car which was practical enough for touring, yet fast enough for competition — not necessarily out-and-out racing, but competition nonetheless. And where there was demand, it followed that there would be supply.

The demand was met by three broad groups of cars divided, for the purposes of this book, into The Grand Marques, Lesser Luminaries, and Minor Classics. The Grand Marques include those makes of car which, by virtue of their pedigree and breeding are securely amongst the aristocrats of the sports car. Here we have manufacturers who never made anything but sports cars (or racing cars) such as Ferrari, Maserati, Porsche, AC, Aston-Martin, Frazer Nash, Lotus, and Morgan, plus a sprinkling who also made touring cars but are perhaps best-known for their sports cars, such as Jaguar, MG, Alfa Romeo, and Mercedes-Benz.

The Lesser Luminaries may be lesser only by dilution. Not all Chevrolets could be called sports cars, but the Corvette certainly was. Equally, one can hardly equate the worthy but relatively rough-and-ready Allard with the Lamborghinis of this world, nor the fading light of Lagonda with the rising stardom of Lotus.

Minor Classics are generally individual models which have become sports cars by reputation or adoption. They include cars such as the Jowett Javelin, that delightfully racy aberration of a traditionally stolid Bradford firm, the Mini-Cooper, the Ford Escort, and the Citroen SM, something of a monument to sporting technology.

Of course, there will be gaps in the sporting repertoire. The requirement that we must consider only road cars precludes the inclusion of, say the Lola T 70. Like the GT 40, the Lola was a sports-racer that could be turned into a road car. Some were, but not as many as the GT 40, so one is included, but not the other. Similarly, some makers who produced road cars in limited numbers have also been excluded on the grounds of space.

A match, at last, for Modena; Ford's V-8 which provided the power for the GT 40, Detroit's reply to the refusal by Enzo Ferrari to team up for a joint assault on Le Mans.

THE DEVELOPING SPORTS CAR 1920-40

New materials, new techniques, new standards of speed and acceleration, better ride and handling, more tenacious road holding, better braking and more power — car designers through the ages sought them all within the constraints of their budgets, or with no regard for expense. Their approach was as diverse as their conclusions. Some lent their creations a metallurgical mystique, creating cars that were as much the product of art as of science. Some simply evolved cars by eradicating their mistakes as best they knew. A few radical engineers avoided preconception, beginning each design with a clear head and a clean sheet.

As Herkomer and Prince Henry were to the Edwardian era, so Le Mans became the breeding ground for the sports cars of the Twenties, Thirties, Forties, and Fifties. Long-distance racing in the idiom of the Grand Prix d'Endurance, the Mille Miglia, the Targa Florio, and the TT, spread eventually across the Atlantic, to Sebring, Bridgehampton, Riverside and Daytona. On the Continent of Europe, the reliability trial developed into the great international rallies such as the International Criterium des Montagnes, the Alpine Rally, or the Monte Carlo Rally, that great mid-winter classic with its scattered starting points. In England, with a determined indifference to speed events on public roads, trials developed differently. Here, the emphasis was laid on climbing muddy hills, to which the small sports cars suited to winding English roads became admirably adapted.

In Germany, the new autobahns encouraged the development of high-speed, streamlined cars with strong

GT car of 1938. The MG 2.6 litre sports saloon may have been no trend-setter, but it followed the fashion of the day with long, flowing lines, a long, high bonnet suggesting plenty of power, and rather small windows. Centre-lock wire wheels were essential for any sporting car — a feature which took a long time to subside.

engines. And as the world recovered from the Depression, sports cars became a symbol of the age.

The Twenties were the Vintage years, when cars appeared to be of such quality that in 1934 a group of enthusiasts met in Harrow, North London to found what became the Vintage Sports Car Club. Aghast at the Fords, Austins and Morrises pouring off the production lines, threatening, it seemed, to engulf them in a sea of motoring mediocrity, they banded together to preserve the 3 litre Bentleys, the 30/98 Vauxhalls, and the 12/50 Alvises, which they treasured in the belief that no worthwhile cars were ever going to be made again.

Fortunately they were wrong. But their example indicates how each generation would regard the art of the sports car as having reached its peak. That little group in Harrow regarded closed cars as somewhat effete, and quiet cars as inconsequential. The car was not made, they imagined, whose chassis did not flex in order to assist road holding. Strong gearboxes capable of taking the power of a big engine required straight-cut gears which needed skill to change at all, let alone change quickly. 'Easy-change' boxes with new-fangled synchromesh would be a sop to the inexpert or the inexperienced.

The classic sports cars of the Vintage era that battled at Le Mans, or crackled over the Apennines (from 1927) on the Mille Miglia were not engineered very

differently from their touring counterparts. Their basis was generally a pressed-steel chassis frame; the engine was at the front, the drive to the rear wheels. Springing was by semi-elliptic leaf springs, sometimes, as on the Lorraine-Dietrich, cantilevered at the rear and occasionally, like the consistent Talbot, quarter-elliptic instead. The engines, in-line fours, sixes, or occasionally eights, were pushrod as a rule, overhead camshaft as an exception.

Roads were still rough, even on racing circuits, and what with flexing chassis, vibrating, often long-stroke engines, and firm springing, supple, wood-framed bodywork was necessary. Closed bodies were tall and heavy — the carriage makers' traditions were still strong, and unitary construction remained strictly for the *avant garde,* such as Lancia, to experiment with. Sports cars remained open cars in the interests of light weight in the first place and less frontal area in the second. Streamlining or, more properly, aerodynamics, was still an inexact science especially when applied to cars. Tall prows abounded; large headlamps and assorted ironmongery in any case made a mockery of any attempt at wind-cheating, until the advent of the fully enclosed body. And that had to wait for chassis and suspension development to ensure it had a firm platform whereon it could be built.

Making reliable cars meant making them sufficiently strong for them not to vibrate or rattle themselves to pieces. Mudguards were a constant source of trouble, forever cracking and tearing off in the course of long races. Most designers could only meet the situation by making chassis frames, wing stays or axles thicker and heavier. That way at least they did not fracture so often, but the weight penalty was severe. It could be countered by large engines, but this often gave a diminishing return.

The great cars of the Vintage era mostly had big engines: the 4,525cc Vauxhall 30/98, the 3,445cc Lorraine-Dietrich, the 2,994cc RL Alfa Romeo, the Bentleys, 3 litres, 4½ litres, and 6½ litres. Cars like these fought out the early Le Mans races, which the Bentleys won in 1924 and 1927-30, challenged by Sunbeam, Lorraine, and in 1929 by the American Stutz with its straight-eight engine and pioneering hydraulic brakes. Yet the prize for technical innovation in this age of giant sports cars must go to the S model Mercedes-Benz, a whole family of cars, the S, SS, SSK, and SSKL,

This streamlined 2.9 Alfa Romeo did more than lead the Le Mans 24 Hours race over the night of June 19/20, 1938. It showed the direction designers would take in enveloping sports cars with efficient low-drag bodywork. Closed sports cars were still rare. When Raymond Sommer passed the pits in the lead for the first time, he waved a Maurice Chevalier-style straw hat to show he was racing in unaccustomed luxury. The car was delayed by a 130 mph blow-out of the right front tyre, the flying tread tearing open the lightweight aluminium body by Touring. The repair can still be seen on the car in the Doune Museum in Scotland.

each faster and more thunderous than the one before, and all derived from the imposing 6.2 litre overhead cam six cylinder touring car designed in 1924 by Ferdinand Porsche.

There were, however, exceptions to the rule of the sporting leviathans. Alfa Romeo, for example, produced the classic 6C 1750 in 1929 with a six cylinder twin overhead camshaft supercharged engine. Its design echoed the valve layout, usually attributed to Ernest Henry, with which Peugot won the 1912 French Grand Prix. Two camshafts, driven in the Peugot's case by a vertical shaft but later more usually by chains, operated the inclined valves directly. For efficiency as well as aesthetic symmetry the design had no equal, and it became the prototype for racing engines and, in time, for production sports car engines as well.

Yet the Vintage years were to pass before such mechanical sophistication was other than exceptional. Most of the giants of the Twenties were either pushrod or single overhead cam apart from the Alfa Romeos, descendants of Vittorio Jano's brilliant P2 Grand Prix car of 1924.

As sports car design entered the 1930s, Alfa Romeo set the pace with the incomparable Type 8C 2300. Here the connection between racing cars and sports cars was at its closest, for the 8C was one of a very few notable cars which could be both, after the fashion of that 1903, 60 hp Mercedes.

With Europe pulling out of a period of great economic difficulty, one car capable of two jobs was a matter of financial as well as engineering expediency. The P2s were seven years old and needed replacement, so it made good sense to build a sports car capable of doubling-up as a Grand Prix car when the occasion demanded. It would need to be versatile, but such a dual personality was still feasible in the early Thirties, before the Mercedes-Benz and Auto Union teams came into Grand Prix racing with their technological overkill.

Jano took some features from the successful little 1750 Alfa such as the cylinder dimensions (65mm stroke and 88mm bore) and made an eight cylinder engine effectively in halves, separated by a train of gears driving the two overhead camshafts and the supercharger. Exquisitely engineered, with

the crankshaft divided and running in no less than ten main bearings, and the cylinder heads made in light alloy with phosphor bronze valve seats, the engine even looked elegant from the outside. The inlet tract was heavily finned in an effort to distribute the heat evenly and to help vaporization of the ingoing mixture from the Memini carburettor at the front, blown by an Alfa-made Roots-type supercharger.

Racing sealed the 8C's reputation. In 1931 it won the Targa Florio, that dramatic race round Sicily which almost matched Le Mans as a sports car classic, and also the Italian Grand Prix, in special short-chassis form. This victory earned it the title 'Monza', and it was to develop into the first true single-seat racing car, the P3 later raced by the Scuderia Ferrari.

As a sports car, the 8C 2300 dominated Le Mans just as the Bentleys had done, with four consecutive victories. It also won the Mille Miglia and Belgian 24 Hours in 1932 and 1933; a bored-out 2,632cc 8C won the Mille Miglia again in 1934.

It was an expensive sports car, but it set the style throughout the Thirties,

with its slim body and cycle-type wings. The windscreen folded flat; racers used small aero screens in front of the driver and mechanic to reduce wind resistance. It was the archetypal sports car of its day, the whippy chassis responding to road shocks which the stiff half-elliptic springs failed to deflect. Capable of up to 115 mph, the entire car came alive with much gnashing of gears and cams, whine from the supercharger, and rasp of exhaust. These were all regarded as a necessary accompaniment to speed; fast cars demanded strong gears, which meant wide, straight-cut teeth meshing firmly together, and such gears were necessarily noisy. It was only later, when mechanical commotion had become less necessary, that the cacophony was eulogized as a concomitant of the sports car.

The role of the 8C Alfa in determining the shape of sports cars to come was emphasized by later versions. The engine was enlarged to 2.9 litres, the chassis made available once again as *Corto* (9ft 2½in) and *Lungo* (9ft 10in) depending on whether it was to be a stripped-down racer, or an elegant coupe by one of the Italian coachbuilders, whose craftsmanship and sense of style came to mean for the sports car what their English counterparts were to the limousine. Zagato, Castagna, and Touring clothed these 2.9 Alfas with some of the most beautifully-proportioned bodies of the time, setting the fashion for the sports two-seater for years to come. And with the value of streamlining, as it was called, at last coming to be recognized, the first fast closed coupes appeared. Nowhere was there more to be gained than at Le Mans, and amongst the prophetic, slippery-looking Adlers in 1938 was one 2.9 Alfa Romeo, the shape of things to come.

Yet sports cars were following the trend of popularization. Motoring for the Masses became a slogan which inspired industrialists and politicians alike, and while the Superleggera Alfa Romeos and the huge Mercedes-Benz S models were setting the fashion (and the pace of the fastest cars in the sporting business) what we may call the 'derived' sports car was making its appearance.

By 'derived' we mean the sports car which takes its mechanical essentials from something else perhaps less sporting. Reverting for a moment to that 1903 example, the Gordon Bennet Mercedes, the touring car and the sports car often had much in common. Maybach's design had laid down principles which would be followed for both sorts for generations — it was the first car to bring together the pattern that was to become so familiar: front engine, rear drive, pushrod overhead valves, close-ratio gearbox with direct top, gate gearchange, pressed steel chassis, honeycomb radiator, forged axles, and so on . . .

Sports cars such as the extravagant Alfas had developed these features and more, but except in America, cars remained for the most part hand-built, and sports cars even more so. What mattered now was to discover what modern sports and touring cars had in common, and use this as a means of reducing the price.

Cars for the well-to-do at the 1928 London Motor Show included the 30/98 Vauxhall Velox at £1,150, the 3 Litre Bentley and 3 Litre Sunbeam for £1,125, while a Morris Cowley cost £177-10s (£177.50). The French were especially adept at small sports cars, Ballot having produced in 1921 probably the first twin overhead camshaft car ever to go into production. The hand of Ernest Henry was apparent in this little 2 litre touring car, derived from the racing Ballots with their 4 cylinder, long-stroke engines and four valves per cylinder. This was an expensive car as well, although it was later joined by the 2LT Ballot with one overhead camshaft, built in larger numbers.

The Alvis 12/50 had made itself a satisfactory reputation with a pushrod engine, and the Amilcar 1100 demonstrated that sports cars need not necessarily be vast, yet there were still few that were cheap. The production of specialized parts in small quantities for short production runs meant that sports cars remained something of a luxury.

It was logical, therefore, to establish the tradition of the sports car which was not bespoke, not exclusive, and not necessarily a plaything of the rich. And the best way to do it was to employ as many parts as possible from cars in series production. It was not enough, of course, simply to do a cosmetic job, to dress up a mass-production car and call it a sports car. It had to have the qualities of performance associated with a sports car. It had to have speed, road-holding, and braking that were out of the ordinary. In these interests, sacrifices of comfort and refinement were cheerfully accepted, and if the whole thing could be made to look a bit dashing, so much the better.

There was less money about in the early Thirties. The Bentley had gone, the Vauxhall 30/98 was no more, nor was the 3 litre Sunbeam. The Alvis Speed Twenty and the Talbot had arrived, more refined than sports cars of the past but still comparatively expensive. The 1½ litre market was contested by Aston Martin and Frazer Nash but just as the squeeze on cash tightened in the grip of the Depression, Cecil Kimber introduced the first in a line of 'derived' cars which were to establish the definitive pattern.

When the first M Type MG Midget appeared in 1930, its resemblance to the ordinary Morris Minor was more than passing. Yet its pedigree was not unlike that of many better-known sports cars, and it suggested to other makers the possibility of taking a promising power unit from a family model and developing it. In this instance, the 847cc four cylinder had an overhead camshaft driven by skew gears from a vertical shaft at the front. This set-up harked back to the days of the post World War I aero-engined monsters, for it had been designed originally by the Wolseley company, who made the Hispano V-8 aero engine with a broadly similar camshaft drive.

Competition led to development of the Midget, together with its companion six cylinder models, the Magna and Magnette, and although by 1936 the ohc Midgets were supplanted by the technically less inviting pushrod TA, the *genre* was established for all time. It came to typify the small British sports car, with stiff springs, spartan bodywork and not much power, which suited English conditions but quickly got out of breath abroad. German cars tended still to be somewhat Wagnerian, while the French, tired of the German and Italian domination of Grand Prix racing, turned with enthusiasm to sports car racing. This led, from 1936, to the development of some very fast sports cars such as the 3.5 litre Delahaye, the Talbot-Lago, and the outstanding Bugatti Type 57. The latter was a 3.3 litre twin overhead camshaft straight eight which won Le Mans in 1936 and 1939, although designed from the outset as a high-quality touring car. Representing the very pinnacle of Bugatti artistry, the light-alloy coupe versions designed by Jean Bugatti were amongst the most beautiful sports cars ever constructed.

Yet technically, sports car design was static. The half-elliptic springs, the willowy frame, the crashing gears, and the whining supercharger were the very stuff of which they were all made. Power was still the principal key to performance; power applied by superchargers, or by large engines — sometimes, as with some highly-regarded English cars such as the Atalanta, Brough Superior, Jensen, and Railton, large American engines, like the 4 litre side-valve Hudson Terraplane.

Other means of obtaining better all-round performance remained largely unexplored. Roadholding was curiously neglected. Hydraulic shock absorbers were coming in gradually, to replace the friction pattern, but independent suspension was still something designers incorporated for comfort rather than speed. Certainly most independent suspensions produced directional stability at best uncertain and at worst wayward. Hydraulic brakes were in their infancy, operating in drums which were getting larger as the increasing importance of good braking was recognized. Drums were finned to assist the dissipation of heat, but except for the bi-metallic drums by then on the horizon, brake design and performance were much the same at end of the Thirties as at the beginning. Engine efficiency had improved certainly, and in 1938 W. O. Bentley's Lagonda V-12 appeared, gaining third place in the final Le Mans before Europe was plunged into conflict. Yet by and large, radical departures from the established order were few and far between. Sports cars remained 'difficult'; it was accepted that they must be firmly sprung, and although steel-reinforced wood chassis had gone out before the First World War, by the time of the Second, many cars still undulated over bumps, their bodies creaking and opening at the seams, just as if the old order had never changed.

Yet it *was* changing. The Italians were producing their extravagantly beautiful coachbuilt masterpieces, the French their matchlessly sculpted engineering works of art, the British their nimble little two-seaters, and the Americans their large-engined, spectacular, and technically promising roadsters. But in Germany, a new order was about to prevail.

Just as Mussolini, for all his shortcomings, was given credit for making the Italian trains run on time, so the public face of National Socialism was one of profound technical achievement, and nowhere was this more apparent than in the field of automotive engineering. These were the days of Dr Porsche and his Volkswagen, of Mercedes-Benz and Auto Union cars sweeping the

board in Grand Prix racing. They were the fledgling days of the Bayerische Motoren Werke which, besides supplying the motive power for a large part of Hitler's Luftwaffe, was also making a sports car which would exert a profound influence and set the visual pattern for most of the next generation of sports cars.

Design radicalism had been left more or less exclusively to Lancia for many years. Trendsetters in the touring car field with the Aprilia and Ardea, which pioneered such advanced features as V-4 engines, inboard brakes and all-independent suspension, Lancia had produced as long ago as 1918 a design for a new style of construction. This was based on the revolutionary idea that the springs and not the car should do the springing. A torsionally stiff frame, that is to say a chassis resistant to twist, Lancia reasoned, together with springing that allowed the wheels to follow the contours of the road, would be more satisfactory than stiff springing and a whippy frame.

Consequently, Lancia developed the so-called monocoque Lambda, and with it the sliding-pillar independent front suspension, which had the unique advantage of keeping the wheel vertical in relation to the road, without the tyre squirming about to accommodate the changes in track or wheelbase as the suspension arms did their job. It was to be many years before the design philosophers in the sports car world caught up with Lancia's train of thought.

In essence, BMW was amongst the first. The BMW 328 evolved from a series of relatively undistinguished touring cars, one of which, the 1½ litre 6 cylinder car, ran in the 1934 Alpine Trial, beating a strong Frazer Nash team and winning the class. This car was in turn a development of the licence-built Austin Seven 'Dixi', with an overhead valve engine and independent front suspension.

The chief engineer, Dr Fritz Fiedler, kept the chassis frame roughly the shape of the Austin, but made it from more convenient tube instead of pressed steel, adding rack and pinion steering while keeping the transverse leaf spring at the front, as the basis for a simple wishbone-type independent suspension along Delahaye-Talbot lines. The engine was modified brilliantly by a consultant engineer named Schleicher in what L.J.K. Setright called the finest performance conversion the business has ever known.

Steel disc wheels, all-enveloping bodies — even a degree of comfort and luxury — revolutionary ideas for a sports car in the late Thirties. But the BMW 328 laid many of the design precepts for the sports car classics of the post-war era. At the wheel, *Autocar's* Midland Editor Ted Eves.

The 2 litre engine had a long lease of life in Bristol cars (see page 51), but so far as BMW was concerned it was destined for a car which was intended for sale and also for racing. The firm saw it as a complement to their competition effort with the famous flat-twin motor cycles. The 328 had a rigid tubular chassis developed from the 1½ litre car, with hydraulic brakes. The 4-speed gearbox had synchromesh on 3rd and top, the shock absorbers were hydraulic, and pierced steel discs were used instead of the traditional wire-spoked wheels.

To offend the sports car traditionalists further, the bodywork was all-enveloping, with integral wings, faired-in headlamps, and a one-piece bonnet hinged forward of the windscreen, opening upwards in the style of the large American cars which the sports enthusiast despised so much. There was even space for carrying luggage.

The BMW 328 was greeted with disbelief. It had relatively soft springing and seemed to disregard all the perceived wisdom of the art and craft of making sports cars. Yet in road trim, with 80 bhp and a weight of under 1,830 lb, it would do 95 mph, and it cost under £700 in Britain, when an Aston Martin of 110 bhp, 2,580 lb and doing 83 mph cost £575 with a lot less style and comfort.

The proof of the pudding lay on the race track. BMW 328s won the 2 litre class in the 1937 Eifelrennen, and the 1938 Mille Miglia. They finished first, second, and third in the 1936 Ulster TT, and won their class again in 1937. They scored class victories in the 1938 Antwerp, Spa 24 Hours, Avus, and Chimay races, and in 1939 at Le Mans and Tobruk-Tripoli. At Brooklands the late and much respected S.C.H. 'Sammy' Davis drove one 102.22 miles in one hour, fully equipped, on pump petrol, with the rev counter reading 4,600-4,900 throughout. In 1939 a lady driver repeated Davis's feat — sports car driving would never be quite the same again.

Thus a revolution was wrought. At the very threshold of the 1940s, sports cars were transformed from doughty ironclads into cars of some poise and refinement. Driving them changed from being a muscular business in which it was necessary to sit close to the wheel, to something a slip of a girl could do, thanks to the accuracy and lightweight feel of the matchless rack and pinion steering. Gearchanging was no longer a highly skilled matching of engine speed and whirling pinions, and the ride over bumps left the fillings in your teeth undisturbed.

In a valedictory appearance at the truncated Mille Miglia race of 1940, BMW produced a team of special cars to contest the 9 laps of a road circuit near Brescia. The winner was a closed coupe which averaged over 100 mph on 130 bhp from the redoubtable 2 litre engine, an object-lesson for the small, efficient cars that would be needed after the war. Open versions of the same car would influence the styling of the new generation of sports cars. But the Fifties would dawn before the world had time to assimilate and put into practice the technical and aesthetic lessons of the Thirties.

Pre-war elegance. Ettore Bugatti's engines were as carefully sculpted as his beautifully proportioned bodywork. Bugatti went to extraordinary lengths to achieve a superlative finish on his engineering.

THE MODERN IDIOM

Following the war, cars were in such short supply that almost anything could be sold. There was little incentive to produce new designs, money for investment in new models was in any case short, materials scarce, and petrol was rationed throughout Europe. The car industries of the Continent were rebuilding, or converting from war work. Sports cars had a low priority.

As a result, completely new designs remained thin on the ground, leaving the market to veterans such as the MG TC with its pushrod engine, pressed steel chassis, non-independent half-elliptic springs, cam and lever steering, ash-framed body, free-standing headlamps and sweeping wings, and rudimentary weather protection. Almost the only concessions to the modernist school were hydraulic brakes and synchromesh on three of the four gears.

Yet the BMW influence *was* to be found. It appeared in the Healey roadsters, rather bulbously interpreting the 1940 line, with Transatlantic overtones, in coupes and roadsters designed with the American market in mind. The establishment of a new trading relationship with the United States had a profound influence on the postwar sports car. Indeed without it, the category might have disappeared altogether. The reasons remain obscure: it might have been the home-going GI, or a more technically-aware postwar generation discriminating against the softly-sprung American cars of the time. Or it might have been the discovery and popularization of road racing in a country traditionally enthused by track, board, and oval racing.

One way or another, MG went, and others followed. For the most part design was not much ahead of MG, but discernible trends gradually emerged. In Italy appropriately, these were chiefly concerned with style. The master artist Pininfarina created a new style and line. To suit America it had to have

Stirling Moss and co-driver
John Cutts driving a
Sunbeam Alpine in the 1954
International Alpine Rally.

certain full-width characteristics — it was not purely an exercise in aerodynamics — but it turned out to be more than simply a selling posture. It emerged as an art-form in many respects, of which a landmark was his Cisitalia of 1948. In France however, faced with a penal taxation system, the sports car went into a period of decline, except in the realm of small, efficient cars, encouraged by a complicated formula at Le Mans which rewarded frugal, streamlined little cars.

Many of the great names of the past had gone, or were in decline. Amilcar dropped out in the early Thirties. Bugatti effectively did not survive the war. Delage and Delahaye struggled on, their days numbered. Isotta-Frashini tried a rear-engined V-8 after the war, but soon disappeared, while in Britain Alvis were making rather mundane tourers, Bentley were making luxury cars, Invicta were making almost nothing, and Singer, Sunbeam and Talbot were for the meantime out of the regular sporting market. In Germany Adler had gone, and Mercedes-Benz and BMW were busy with a matter of survival.

The seller's market encouraged new makes of sports car to appear. One was Allard of whom it is not being ungenerous to say that their entrepreneurial skill probably exceeded their technical capability. The cars were primarily trials machines, bred for ascending muddy hills, a sport almost unknown outside England. With smart bodywork they found a market in the late Forties and even went on to distinguish themselves at Le Mans and in the Monte

Carlo Rally, but against strengthening competition from the likes of Jaguar, who grasped the new technology, most of the new wave of enterprising car makers disappeared.

Some however did not. With the platform chassis of the humble Volkswagen as a basis, Porsche started production of a series of the world's most distinguished sports cars. Ferrari had made cars before the war, but only began serious production afterwards. The great days of many well-established names such as AC and Triumph were still to come. Personalities abounded in the postwar world, like 'The Sorcerer' himself, Amédée Gordini; yet who would have guessed that

Perhaps the most celebrated postwar sports car, the Jaguar XK 120:

By the postwar years, the sporting reputation of Alvis was fading. Nevertheless the 3 litre coupe, which ceased production in 1967, was a fine touring car.

The Jaguar XK engine, still basically unchanged after more than 30 years.

right and far right
The ancestor of all Ferrari V-12s, the Colombo-designed Type 166. Single overhead camshaft, hairpin valve springs, twin magnetos, and three carburettors made in the factory of Ferrari's old friend Eduardo Weber. The 166 was the first production version of the original 125, the designation marking the change in cylinder capacity from 125cc to 166cc, bringing the engine to a full 2 litres. The sparse nature of the bodywork enabled the 166 to be used on the road or for racing.

some of the greatest sports cars of future years were going to come not from Molsheim, Milan, Coventry, or Stuttgart, but from the burgeoning technology of America, a country capable of creating an entire industry to fly men to the moon? Making a sports car with the right feel and balance, the right looks and the right traditions was no less mean a feat. Even Japan got into the act,

appropriately with a sports car destined to become a world best seller.

So far as technique went, however, the legacy of BMW took time coming through. Donald Healey and his engineer A. C. Sampietro were amongst the first to appear with fresh thoughts on sports car design, using a rather expensive trailing link independent front suspension on their first cars, which were very clearly in the more civilized BMW mould. One of the prototype engines under study at Jaguar was designated XG, and had a BMW-style cross-pushrod system providing hemispherical combustion chambers from a single low camshaft, after the fashion of Schleicher. But it was a classic twin overhead camshaft design *à la* Henry which Jaguar adopted.

Torsion bar independent suspension was used on the Jaguar and, as soon as they were available, disc brakes, but the XK 120 had a straightforward chassis, a twin-channel pressed steel frame, with a live axle on semi-elliptic springs at the rear. Yet chassis design was the next major step forward in the story of the sports car.

BMW had realized there was more to performance than power. They had

exemplified the philosophy that a stiff chassis and supple springs would improve cornering — it was easy to make up a power deficiency, if one existed, by simply going faster round the corners. Furthermore the aircraft industry had already worked out a number of ways of making a structure which was both light in weight and relatively rigid under both beam and torsional stresses.

Simple ladder frames of tubular construction quickly found favour with firms such as Ferrari and AC. Seamless tube was easy to obtain and easy to work. There was no need for expensive heavy tools for bending or forming, and brackets, uprights, and sub-frames could be welded or bolted on quite easily. Welding techniques had improved during the war, and there was little fear of cars shaking themselves to pieces owing to brittle welds, or deterioration of the surrounding metal.

It was left to Mercedes-Benz to take another leaf out of the aircraft designer's book and build up a chassis of small diameter tubes. For their 300 SL they designed a carefully triangulated framework following once again the principle of making a car with a stiff frame

and softer springs, by now considered essential for improving road holding. On many subsequent so-called 'space frames' the difficulties of making apertures for installing major items, such as the engine, were solved by making some tubes, vital in supporting the triangulation, bolt in place instead of being welded. They could thus be replaced and taken out again every time it was necessary to change the engine.

Once again improvements in welding contributed to advances in design, and the days of the old-style chassis frame, with its brackets and sub-frames bolted or rivetted to it, appeared to be numbered. Yet a third form of construction was the platform chassis such as Porsche adopted from Volkswagen. This was a raft made up of steel pressings on which the body could be mounted by spot-welding — literally welding in spots and not continuously along the seams where two pressings join.

One logical stage further than this, of course, was to take Lancia's principle of 1920 and make the car as a whole, from small pieces of sheet steel pressed to shape and welded to form what is usually called a monocoque hull.

Cradled in a space-frame of small-gauge tubes, an early Cosworth-adapted Ford engine powers the sports-racing Lotus 23. The reclining back of the seats put the driver in a reclining posture which kept the height of the car down.

Now the true monocoque, or stressed skin structure, is exemplified by an egg, and openings to get things out (or put them in) weaken it. Accordingly a car monocoque structure is necessarily complex, requiring either much hand-work making individual panels, or a battery of heavy presses for making quantity.

What this boils down to is that sports car design came to depend very heavily on rather more than plain performance. Designers had to ask themselves how many examples were to be built, what they were to cost, and what components, or bought-in items, were to hand. The entire equation became more complex,

and the designers' answers were as varied as their problems. Some chose to incorporate a number of different techniques, such as Jaguar when they came to build the D-Type and E-Type. The centre and rear of the chassis was a monocoque, while the front part was a sub-frame made up of welded square and round-section tubes.

With varied means available of providing a strong, rigid chassis, and the principle of softer springing accepted, there came greater freedom in suspension design. Swing axles came to be regarded as a fairly primitive form of independent suspension, even though they had been used by Dr Porsche for his

The 300SL's tubular space-frame is shown in this cutaway drawing which reveals why the gull-wing doors were necessary. Ordinary doors would not have been big enough to allow the occupants to get in and out in an emergency. This is the racing prototype with two spare wheels in the tail, and a smaller cockpit turret top than later production versions.

early Auto Union racing cars. For as tyres grew wider, the obvious shortcomings of camber change and decrease in track became apparent, and the system became largely discredited. Lancia's goal of keeping the tyre vertical to the road was aimed at in a variety of ways, and beam axles for sports car front suspension were soon on the way out. It was many years, however, before fully-independent rear suspension was accepted as the general rule. De Dion, which is something in-between, with the differential fixed to the chassis, and the rear wheels linked by a tube round the back keeping them upright, found some favour with, amongst others, Allard on the J2. It was a sophisticated arrangement, especially on this car, which retained the somewhat anomalous swing axles on the front.

Probably the first all-independent sports car put into production in any quantity was the AC Ace. John Tojeiro, who designed the car, had seen how effective the Cooper 500cc racing cars were in adapting Fiat 500 front suspensions at both ends. Using a similar transverse upper leaf spring and lower wishbone arrangement at front and rear of his simple ladder-type tubular frame, he was able to provide a singularly effective all-independent sports car capable of being produced in limited numbers economically. It was a tribute to his ingenuity that the design not only

survived quite a long time, but coped, for a time at any rate, with massive increases in power as the V-8 Cobra supplanted the six cylinder.

Sports car design never really settled down the way small car design did — the requirements were so varied. So while the world, clear in its need for economy and roominess in its Minis, could find no better formula than Sir Alec Issigonis' east-west engine and front wheel drive, the sports car designer trying to satisfy so many conflicting interests could discover no such common ideal.

Aerodynamics and structural requirements between them were responsible for the increasing number of sports cars with fixed roofs. The better drag figures noticed on the Mulsanne straight before the war spoke for themselves, and the provision of an open cockpit, making a large hole in space frame structures, became inconvenient. A roof solved both problems at a stroke, and making sacrifices in comfort for the sake of speed became unnecessary. Open cars did not disappear of course, for such is the diversity of the sports car market that to many customers, the wind in the hair and the sun in the face is part and parcel of the whole business.

Engines tended to remain at the front of sports cars until the mid-sixties. Only Porsche really mastered the technique of making a sports car with the engine at the back, and even that remains the

Enlarging the engine of the Jaguar E-Type from 3.8 litres to 4.2 litres in 1964 brought a number of improvements. An all-synchromesh gearbox meant less grating of the rather heavy gearchange, but the cars were no faster — indeed the process of weight-gain and unnecessary embellishment which afflicted so many splendid cars had already begun.

overleaf
Racing car under wraps. The Jaguar XJ 13 was built as a Le Mans contender, with a four-cam version of the Jaguar V-12 behind the driver. Its very existence was denied by Jaguar for years, until they revealed they had intended to race it in 1966-67 before their plans were disrupted by the BMC amalgamation. It would almost certainly have remained competitive up till the arrival of the Porsche 917, and was superior in performance to late developments of the Ford GT 40.

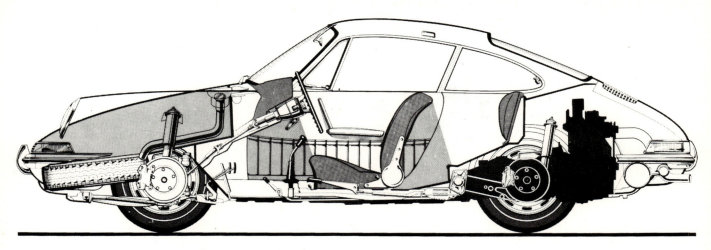

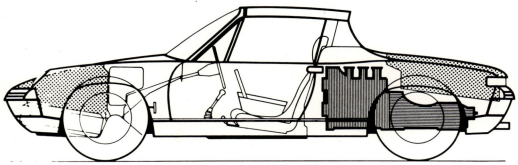

subject of a good deal of argument. But as racing cars began putting the engine behind the driver yet ahead of the rear wheels, thus becoming mid-engined as opposed to rear-engined, it was inevitable that sports cars should follow suit.

The mid-engined movement in racing began to gather pace in 1955, when Jack Brabham entered a mid-engined Cooper — effectively an adaptation of a Cooper sports car — in the British Grand Prix. The Coopers, Charles and his son John, had come into racing through the 500cc racing car movement. Driving the rear wheels by means of a chain after the practice of the motor cycles from which the engines came, the middle was the logical place for them: the cars were so small and light they had little effect on weight distribution in any case.

When they came to make sports cars, with the exception of the front-engined Cooper-Bristol, the Coopers stuck to their mid-engined guns partly at least because they had come to know a great deal about them. So, when they came to build a sports car with full-width bodywork, tubular frame, and short Kamm tail, they put the engine behind the driver. With a Bristol engine (that 328 BMW derivative again) Brabham entered a modified version of the sports car with a central seating position in the Grand Prix, starting a revolution in

Formula 1 racing which culminated in his world championships of 1959 and 1960.

A shift towards mid-engined cars in sports car racing followed, making the watershed between road-going sports cars and track-going sports cars distinct. Yet the mid-engined concept did eventually apply itself to road cars as well. The first such design to go into production was the Lotus Europa in 1966; subsequently Porsche produced the 914 and Matra the 530, none of which was very fast, but all of which demonstrated that for the ultimate in cornering and road holding, the layout was without equal. Henceforward, sports cars of any other configuration would be considered compromises. Once again, some sacrifices had to be made for performance — not this time discomfort through having no roof, but in terms of passenger and luggage space. Fiat's X1/9 and the Matra-Simca Bagheera and its sucessor the Talbot Matra Murena solved the space problem better, but mid-engines as a rule did not offer as much habitation within the car as front engines.

Transverse engines, air-cooled engines, five speed gearboxes, fuel injection, turbochargers and superchargers, glass reinforced plastic monocoques and body panels, back-bone chassis frames, saloons, coupes, 2+2s, Targa tops and folding hoods — all the jargon

Rear-engined and mid-engined. The traditional rear-engined Porsche 912 *(top)*, a short-lived flat-four car introduced together with the 911, carries its engine behind the centre-line of the rear axle. Luggage goes into the shaded area at the front, and behind the seats. The unsuccessful Porsche 914 *(lower picture)* is mid-engined, with the mass of the cylinder block ahead of the rear axle, and the carburettor intakes just behind the driver's head. Luggage space is still at a premium; room was found in the nose and above the transmission.

Pininfarina saved 100 Kg over the standard Audi Quattro by styling the Quattro Quartz, a special version with a steel/polypropylene sandwich laminate for the doors, bumper sections made from Kevlar and honeycomb sandwich, fibre epoxy resin for rear window frame, seat frames and steering wheel, and Lexan polycarbonate for the rear window itself. Pininfarina's mastery of production techniques made him the engineer's coachbuilder.

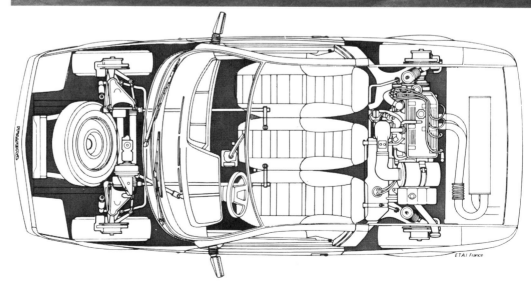

Matra's solution to the space problem in mid-engined cars — three-abreast seating and a transverse engine. This is the Murena.

of the sports car provides a wealth of variety and ingenuity. Yet the prospects for the rest of the Eighties may be less promising than the past. Rather like the enthusiasts who met in Harrow in 1934 and decided that their own special sort of car was not being built after 1930, their Orwellian counterparts in 1984 could reach a similar decision.

If 1930 saw the end of the Vintage era, and the Thirties the Post-Vintage Thoroughbreds, what of the Forties and Fifties? Here was the age of the classics, perhaps. In the Sixties and Seventies came the supercars, the Ferraris and Porsche 928s. But those dreary contra-dictory economic twins, inflation and depression, those multiplying oil prices,

and those encroaching legislators still have the sports car under threat. It is a comforting thought that there are so many of them still in use that, short of a programme of mass destruction, sports cars will remain with us for the foresee-able future even should their manu-facture be suddenly outlawed on a worldwide basis. Sports motoring, like hunting and shooting, has survived disapproval and antipathy. Like climb-ing or boxing, it has dodged the do-gooders. Safety has its place in every sporting scheme of things, and the road is not necessarily the place for feats of skill and daring, yet the spice and glamour of the sports car will continue to prevail.

THE GRAND MARQUES

AC

AC Cars, as if time had passed them by, restarted production after the war with a design which harked back not just to the immediate pre-war period, but to 1919, when John Weller's famous light-alloy 1,991cc single overhead camshaft wet-liner six cylinder engine was unveiled at the London Motor Show.

It said a great deal for it that it lasted so long — it did not go out of production until 1963. But the rather lugubrious saloon in which AC installed it when they resumed production in 1947 was obviously not going to remain in the automotive mainstream when the market returned to normal.

AC engaged the services of John Tojeiro, whose designs for sports-racing cars seemed to work, and who had been

hired by Charles and John Cooper to plan their only front-engined production car, the Cooper-MG. Tojeiro's formula was simple. His ladder-type frame consisting of two 3in diameter tubes, with independent suspension, accommodated the Weller engine in much the same way as a similar design had accommodated a four cylinder MG. The body style was cribbed without much alteration, and certainly no acknowledgement, from a contemporary Ferrari, the old AC gearbox was used, and the car was marketed as the Ace.

It was an immediate success. The frame was stiff, and the handling was sensational for 1953 — it would remain good ten years later. A coupe version known as the Aceca was added to the range, and by a process of steady evolution an excellent, intuitive sort of design only improved. Disc brakes were included when they became available, but with a top speed only just over 100 mph, the power was insufficient to exploit the excellent road holding. As an alternative to the old 102 bhp engine, AC offered the Bristol (née BMW) 2 litre with 125 bhp, which gave both models well over 115 mph.

By 1961 however, Bristol had discontinued the engine, and the alternative was a rather unsatisfactory modified Ford Zephyr pushrod power unit with 170 bhp, but little refinement and great weight.

Driven into seventh place at Le Mans in 1963 by Ninian Sanderson and Peter Bolton, this AC Cobra was tested by the author on the MIRA banking, where it achieved 139.6 mph on the timing strip between corners. At Le Mans it did over 160 mph at 5,500 rpm on Mulsanne, with the help of the semi-streamlined hardtop.

opposite
The clean lines of the 1962 AC Ace owe more to the contemporary Ferrari than to English domestic styling. Removable sidescreens were becoming outmoded, with even the cheapest sports cars acquiring winding windows. The Cobra employed the same basic shape, with bulges to accommodate the larger engine and bigger wheels.

Help fortunately was at hand. The Cavalry arrived in the best Western tradition, led by the colourful Texan Carroll Shelby. The first Cobra prototype was built in 1962, basically an Ace chassis suitably altered to take a Ford V-8 engine, with wider tyres and body modifications to cope with what finally turned out to be more than twice the horse power of the Ace Zephyr.

For sheer bravura, few cars would ever match a well-tuned Cobra. There were two models, one with a 4.2 or 4.7 litre V-8, then from the middle of 1965 a 7 litre giving up to 345 bhp in road trim and a top speed around 145 mph, along with immensely strong acceleration. The standing quarter-mile could be covered in under 13 seconds.

Performance of this order, however, made immense demands on the chassis, and changes had eventually to be wrought. Rack and pinion steering was one of the first. It is curious how many designs carried over from the Thirties continued using old steering systems, with drop-arms and drag links, at least until the inclination of rack and pinion arrangements to lock-up at inconvenient moments was curbed. The Cobra's suspension had be be changed as well, combined coil spring and damper layouts with wishbones replacing the transverse leaf springs.

The Cobra went under a lot of names. Sometimes the AC part was dropped altogether; it was known as a Shelby Cobra, a Shelby American, and sometimes

above
Cockpit and engine of the Cobra Le Mans coupe illustrated on the previous page. The dashboard features a non-standard arc-type tachometer. With a carburettor choke per cylinder, the car managed 8 mpg in the race.

right
Stylish Italian body on the Cobra was by Frua. A coupe version was also available.

as a Ford Cobra. AC provided it with a Frua body and called it simply the 428, a stylish but not very successful model which formed the firm's sole exhibit for several years at the London Motor Show long after production had effectively ceased.

Yet AC were determined to carry on making cars. Once again however, they had to call upon outside help. In order to meet the competition, they were obliged to look towards a mid-engined coupe, and they found this in a one-off design exercise in 1972, drawn up by Robin Stables and Peter Bohanna. This was the Diablo, in which an Austin Maxi engine and transmission had been cleverly adapted to drive the rear wheels instead of the front. Lying across the frame, the overhead cam engine fitted neatly behind the seats of a compact if somewhat lumpish reinforced plastic body.

It took until 1979 for AC to put the car on the road. The first oil crisis made the market look uncertain, and there were serious difficulties in developing the model for production. The Maxi engine turned out to be unsuitable, so a 3 litre Ford Capri V-6 had to be used instead, with a five speed gearbox made by AC with Hewland gears. Then, just as the 3000ME as it was known, reached the market, the second oil crisis struck . . .

Instead of the 40 or so cars a week that may have seemed likely at the beginning of the decade, AC found themselves making perhaps three in a good week.

Alfa Romeo

The successors to the legendary 2.9s and the lithe 1750s have been nothing if not mixed. They have not all been sports cars, and it is probably just as well that some of them made no pretence about the matter. Yet for the most part they have carried on the traditions of well-mannered handling and sporting style established by one of the most famous names in racing. They have also contrived to echo down the years those satisfactory mechanical noises which contribute to so many sporting drivers' enjoyment — the mellifluous clatter of overhead cams popping the valves open and snapping them shut again, and the solid, reassuring feel of a gear lever which changes gears as fast as you can move your wrist.

Production volumes at Alfa had never been high, but the firm, nationalized in 1933, had new priorities after the war. Their stroke of genius was the Giulietta (Romeo and Giulietta — does the connection register?). As soon as their postwar saloon range was safely on the road, they set about something completely new: a twin overhead camshaft engine of 1,290cc which revved to well over 6,000 rpm and gave 80 bhp. The camshafts were chain driven, the stiff crankshaft ran in five bearings, and each of the four gears was equipped with synchromesh and changed exquisitely. The rear axle was located by

Pretty name for a pretty car. The Giulietta by Alfa Romeo. The Pininfarina two-seat Spyder fixed the pattern for many sports cars of the era, with its fine detail and elegant proportions, and was in production from 1954 to 1963. Bertone did the two-door Coupe; this 1961 Spyder is by Pininfarina.

The pert prettiness of the Giulietta was not an easy act to follow, as the rather exaggerated lines of the Bertone Giulia Sprint Speciale demonstrate.

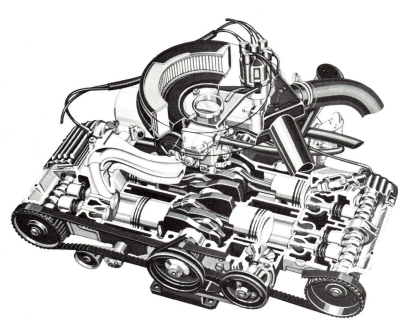

Alfa's Boxermotor. With the connecting rods fighting one another, boxer-fashion, the Alfasud flat-four has its cylinders horizontally opposed VW-fashion. Visible in this cutaway view are the overhead camshafts driven by toothed belt, and the rather long inlet tract from the single carburettor shown here. Sporting Alfasuds had more direct induction.

radius arms and a centrally pivoted A-bracket. Giulietta Sprints had 90 horse power and a two door body of such perfect proportions that it made most other cars on the road (and not a few succeeding Alfas) appear clumsy and overweight.

Bertone styled the little coupe and its companion Spyder open two seater. It was to remain one of the world's most beautiful cars from its introduction in 1953 until replaced by the Giulia series in 1963. It was lively rather than fast, and held the road well, although not all of its derivatives were as commendable. The Giulietta SS, or Sprint Speciale, did over 120 mph, but although it used much the same floor pan, the weight distribution went wrong and the Bertone version never seemed to have the road grip which gave the lighter Zagato a number of worthy rally victories in the early 1960s.

The Giulietta was a difficult act to follow, but the Giulia proved up to it. It was 1964, however, before the design came into its own, in particular the Sprint GTA and GTV, styled, like its predecessor, by Bertone, and equipped with engines up to 2 litres giving a top speed of 120 mph in the fifth of its gears. A convertible of less elegant lines known as the Duetto or Giulia Spyder was also available.

Overlapping the end of the Giulietta and the beginning of the Giulia in the early Sixties, the Giulia Tubolare Zagato, which proved so successful in rallies and long-distance sports car races (the Giulia TZ), was rather less of a road car and more of an out-and-out racer. Like so many sporting and competition cars of the era, it was stripped down to its essentials to reduce weight; trim, upholstery, and sound deadening were either removed or, in the TZ's case, never installed. The noise inside was deafening. The 'Tubolare' came from the tubular chassis frame of the TZ, which was built in limited numbers and capable of well over 140 mph.

Alfa Romeo carried out an immensely successful racing programme throughout the Thirties. Yet even they were eventually overwhelmed by the might of Mercedes-Benz and Auto Union in what was known as Formula A, Grand Prix racing. With a sense of exasperation, they turned to the next class down, known as Voiturette, which had an engine capacity limitation of 1½ litres supercharged. For this Ing. Colombo designed a Grand Prix car in miniature, a straight-eight single seater with a rounded front and a pointed tail, expected to carry all before it in the last two seasons of racing before the war.

It very nearly did. The Germans produced a rival in secret, and the Alfa

Romeo 158 failed to win its first race in Tripoli, but it was eligible for the premier formula after the war. The team of cars had been hidden for the duration, emerging unbeaten in Grandes Epreuves from 1946-48, and again from 1950 until the middle of 1951, when the big Ferrari at last overtook them.

The Little Alfas were called 'Alfettas', and the name was passed on to a new range of road cars in 1967. They kept the customary Alfa Giulia twin-cam four cylinder engine, but in an effort to distribute the weight more equably, the five speed gearbox was built into the final drive over the rear axle. The suspension at the back was by de Dion, with radius arms and a Watts linkage which, together with the extra weight on the driving wheels, gave the Coupe and Sprint models immense traction. The styling was new as well — not by Bertone as most other post-war Alfas had been, but by a former Bertone employee who had decided to set out on his own, and who would wield even more influence on the shape of many cars to come — Giorgetto Giugiaro.

Alfa Romeo's position in the social structure of the country was emphasized in 1971, when the firm found itself more or less instructed to set up a new factory, making a small car, in the south of Italy, an area of chronic unemployment.

Giugiaro had a hand in the new model, known, because of the location of the new plant, as the Alfasud.

It turned out to be no ordinary economy car. Like almost every Alfa, it maintained the make's tradition for roadworthiness, and remained probably the best-handling small car in the world. Its flat-four engine and front wheel drive lent themselves to a sporting application, putting the Alfasud Sprint and certain Lancia models in a unique position amongst the Grand Marques as front wheel drive sports cars.

Alfasuds began life with a modest 1,186cc, but the engine was enlarged to provide the Sprint Veloce with 1,490cc, giving up to 105 mph and the best part of 28 miles per Imperial gallon. Once again it was a car which scored heavily though not so much through being extremely fast — compared with many sports cars it was not. But it could be steered with almost breathtaking precision, placed on the road exactly where the driver wanted to go, with very little body roll and a flat, even ride which went a long way to make up for the rather mean-looking interior. And even the usual Alfa Romeo mechanically musical noises remained — the 'Sud's little 'boxer' engine produced a delightfully discreet little rasping exhaust note.

The inimitable Tubolare', the Alfa Romeo Giulia TZ with lightweight shell of a body by Zagato for racing.

Clean lines and good proportions. The crisp good looks of the DB2 Aston Martin set the pattern for a postwar classic which pursued glory on the race track and gathered prestige for tractor magnate David Brown.

Aston Martin

Even the firm's staunchest admirers concede that the commercial history of Aston Martin has been at best chequered. Reaching the brink of failure in the wake of successive oil crises was nothing new. Its founders of 1914, Lionel Martin and Robert Bamford, having set up Bamford and Martin Ltd in 1922, were forced to wind it up by 1925. But the firm's racing reputation carried it forward under the direction of A. C. Bertelli, then R. G. Sutherland until 1948, when control passed into the hands of David Brown, the tractor tycoon.

The acquisition by David Brown was significant technically as well as commercially, because he had recently bought Lagonda as well, which made available the twin overhead cam 2½ litre engine designed for Lagonda by W. O. Bentley. Aston had already started racing, and the Claud Hill-designed, essentially pre-war 2 litre driven by St John Horsfall won its class in the 1946 Belgian Grand Prix. A new car with Hill's pushrod 2 litre engine, independent front suspension, and traditional open bodywork with separate wings, was built in an astonishingly short time for Horsfall and Leslie Johnson to win

the Spa 24 hours race. Encouraged, the new owner embarked on a programme of racing with the aim of producing a range of sports and GT cars to match the best from the Continent.

The new 2½ litre engine was vital, and it was installed in a multi-tube chassis with sleek two-door closed bodywork just in time to appear at the first postwar Le Mans. This was the DB2 (the DB1 was a somewhat bulbous open car with the pushrod engine), which formed the basis for a successful series of cars including the DB2/4, one of the world's first hatchbacks, in which the rear window opened to provide access to the luggage space, and the racing DB3 and DB3S, with a chassis by Dr Eberan von Eberhorst, the pre-war Auto Union designer.

The road manners of these Astons were, for their time, impeccable. They were good looking and exclusive, certainly Britain's best sports car of the immediate postwar period. The DB3S, with its carefully sculpted front and flared, cutaway wings, became one of the great classic sports cars, commanding high prices on the collectors' market.

Turning his attention to Grand Prix racing proved a brief and expensive adventure for David Brown, but Aston

As time went by, weight and complication set in, as was the custom, and while the silhouette remained much the same, the appearance became altogether fussier and less satisfactory. Yet the DB2/4 Aston had one prophetic feature — the back window opened, giving access to the luggage space, making it one of the world's pioneer hatchbacks.

A development of the DB3, the DB3S Aston Martin was shorter, lighter, and better looking. The chassis was the work of Eberan von Eberhorst, and the Bentley-designed six-cylinder engine was developed to provide 180bhp with three twin-choke Weber carburettors.

A development of the elegant DB3S, the brutish looking DBR1/300 scored a convincing victory at Le Mans after ten years unremitting effort by David Brown. The Roy Salvadori/ Carroll Shelby car won, followed by the Maurice Trintignant/Paul Frère car, after team manager John Wyer sent Stirling Moss out to break up the opposition. The DBR1 brought the world sports car championship to Britain in 1959, the first year of Jack Brabham's two world Formula 1 titles with Cooper-Climax.

remained successful in sports car racing with the space-framed and de Dion-axled DBR series. These appeared with 2.5 litre, 2.9 litre, and 3.7 litre engines, won the Nurburgring 1000 Kilometre race three years in a row, the Spa 24 Hours in 1957, scored a 1-2-3 victory in the 1958 TT, and came first and second at Le Mans in 1959, when they won the World Sports Car Championship.

Thereafter, Aston's interest in racing declined, but in 1958 they introduced the DB4, with the new twin-cam 3.7 litre engine. It began stylishly enough, with an elegant Superleggera body, but practicality and fashion dictated the rounding-off which accompanied the DB4GT. The most spectacular of the series was the DB4GT Zagato, of which only 25 were made, mostly for racing. These could do well over 150 mph and with a massive 315 horse power in racing trim, heavy steering, and rather ponderous gearbox, they were cars which required a good deal of muscle as well as nerve to drive fast.

Between 1959 and 1963, over 1,100 DB4s were built, followed by the DB5, which amalgamated the long DB4 body with the rounded nose of the GT. This version in turn was lengthened and be-spoilered, and the David Brown gearbox at last gave way to a rather more manageable ZF, but the light, elegant lines had gone, the car had grown

above
Tall, upright six cylinder engines with two overhead camshafts provided the power for all the David Brown Aston Martins.

Carefully-sculpted razor-edged styling by William Towns suited the DBS Aston Martin admirably. The first V-8 models grew some necessary lumps and intakes, but later versions spoilt the crisp appearance, even to the extent of blanking off radiators when research revealed very little air had time to get through at over 120 mph.

The Bentley conception had given way to an altogether larger power unit by the time of the Aston Martin DB4, the lighter and shorter version of which was the racing DB4GT *(bottom)* of which less than 100 were ever made. With over 300bhp, they could do over 150mph, and reach 100 in 20 seconds. Even more raceworthy, the beautiful Zagato version *(top)* — a pinnacle of Aston Martin's development as a sports car.

heavy, and it was no longer in the sporting *avant garde,*

A new model was on the way however, and although it was to follow a similar path, adding weight and losing elegance as the years passed, world events of the early Seventies were to prove more significant than anything that happened in the tiny works at Newport Pagnell, where the cars were made.

The DBS in six cylinder form was probably the best looking of all the DB Aston Martins and represented the English GT car at the summit of its development. Styled by William Towns, it looked a match for anything else in the world — not by apeing rival designs so much as by adopting a distinctive, somewhat understated look of its own. Longer and wider than the DB5 and the DB6 which preceded it, although using much the same structure, the DBS

was smooth, fast, and built with all the coachbuilt care of the best luxury cars.

Alas, more power was decreed, and a large, heavy V-8 which took over-long to develop was squeezed in. The customary disfigurement followed, and Aston Martin seemed no longer able to match the great Continental marques such as Ferrari or Lamborghini in terms of either style or engineering. Hand-built quality remained their principal stock-in-trade, and when the world plunged into crisis in 1973, it was not enough.

In 1972 the David Brown Group had in any case sold Aston Martin to Company Developments Ltd, the first of a number of changes in ownership during the Seventies. The V-8 was re-engineered to produce the sort of power it should have turned out when new, (although like Rolls-Royce, the firm is traditionally coy about saying exactly how much it does turn out) and the car would reach 170 mph in impressive silence. At this speed air dams and spoilers become necessary, and the more powerful Vantage version was distinguished by having the front intake blanked off completely after the engineers discovered that the rather blunt aerodynamics swept most of the air straight past anyway.

Under the regime of Alan Curtis, who rescued the firm along with Peter Sprague in 1975, development was concentrated on a new Lagonda of striking design, incorporating a number of advanced and extremely complicated electronic systems.

BMW

While Bristol held the pioneering 328 BMW in trust, as it were, elevating it to the status almost of a cult, but hardly making a great commercial success out of it, BMW after the war were faced with the complete reconstruction of their business, their principal plant and assets being irretrievably lost on the wrong side of the Iron Curtain. They made a notable success of it nevertheless.

They were forced at first to make some rather undignified economy cars, and would probably rather forget their mercifully short-lived Isetta bubble car, but they entered the small sports car market in 1959 with the 700 series, small two-door coupes which started life with an air-cooled flat-twin engine from the economy 600 model. Compared with their glorious past, it must have seemed an unpromising stage on the way to recovery, but despite almost two-thirds of the car's weight being on the rear wheels, it handled surprisingly well. A young Belgian, Jacky Ickx, began racing one on his way to fame and fortune.

In an effort to keep their spirits up, however, BMW still made a few big cars in the form of the voluptuous 501, with a 2 litre engine based on the pre-war six cylinder Schleicher adaptation. For the relatively modest power the car was too large and heavy, and a V-8 of 2.6 litres

was developed. Enlarged to just over 3 litres this pushrod design was installed in the 507, an elegant and stylish 140 mph GT two seater which was made in open and closed forms.

But by the mid Sixties, BMW policy had changed. They invested heavily in a new range of cars coming between their expensive prestige products and their economy runabouts. The floor pressings for this new range formed the basis for new sporting coupes, the 2000 CS and the 2800 CS.

The bodies were made by the coachbuilding firm of Karmann, and in the case of the six cylinder 2800 required more than simply taking the bottom half of a saloon and putting a new top on. Quite extensive re-engineering was needed to produce cars which, although they looked rather heavy at the front in 1965 form, were fast (up to 120 mph) and established BMW firmly amongst the best-handling middle-class cars in Europe.

The firm's return to racing in the image of the 328 only came with the 3 litre model of 1971. This was the 3.0CS which, with fuel injection added, became the 3.0CSi, combining clean, light looks, and a 140 mph performance. Smooth and quiet, it quickly became popular as an outstanding touring car despite a formidable price.

Many of the best sports cars only achieved greatness through evolution, however, and as with the 328, the six

overleaf
Supercar of the Eighties. BMW M1, one of the last great mid-engined designs of what has been called the second Vintage era. Styled by Giugiaro, raced by the Grand Prix aces in the Procar series, the M1 sped BMW back into top-flight competition.

The shapely BMW 2800CS of 1968 put the Bavarian make firmly back in the GT market. Performance remained modest, with a top speed little more than 110mph.

Hans Stuck with the BMW 3.0 CSL (3½ litres, 430bhp), at the Nurburgring during his record lap of 8 min 10.9 sec. Stuck raced BMWs with great enthusiasm and success in long-distance events and the 1978 Procar series.

cylinder BMW coupes of the Seventies really came alive following the development of lightweight bodies and 24-valve cylinder heads. In time, fins and spoilers came as well, and the 3.0 CSL (C for *Coupe*, S for *Sport*, L for *Leicht*) dominated touring car racing, even against the formidable works Ford Capris, until they were withdrawn in 1975.

In racing, the turbocharged era was yet to come, and BMW coupes grew in speed and power rather closer to the idiom of the thunderous Mercedes-Benz SSK of 45 years before, than the lissome 328. Yet the most potent BMW was still to come.

Bavaria's contribution to the supercar category dated from the final days of the CSL. The war with Ford for the European Touring Car Championship was over, with honour satisfied on both sides. BMW, for marketing and engineering reasons, turned instead towards sports racing cars. Their aim, however, was to make a car which, rather like Ford and their GT 40, could be sold in limited numbers for road use.

The M1 coupe had a difficult gestation. The engine was already available — the twin cam, 24-valve six cylinder from the CSL, now a full 3½ litres. But the M1 was to be a mid-engined design with a multi-tube chassis, and construction was to be in the hands of Lamborghini — well accustomed to such work in small numbers.

Alas, Lamborghini had troubles of their own, crippled by the growing world depression. Eventually, the chassis was built by a sub-contractor in Modena; likewise the glass-reinforced plastic body was styled (by Giugiaro) and built in Italy.

In road form the M1, with 277 bhp, would do 130 mph in fourth gear, and over 160 mph in top. The model was adopted in 1979 for the Procar series of races run in conjunction with world championship Grands Prix, partly as a BMW publicity exercise, and partly it might be supposed to find some sort of gainful employment for the production run of 400 cars, for which the manufacturers were finding buyers in short supply. For racing, this remarkable 3,453cc engine could provide up to 500 horse power, giving the car, with suitable gearing, a potential of well over 200 mph, while a turbocharged version was also available, capable of turning out a staggering 850 bhp.

Amongst the supercars, the BMW M1 was in a class of its own, and although in many respects it was a racing car, it was produced in sufficient quantity to qualify it, according to international rules, as a production car. Thus it should not be confused with those immensely powerful (up to 1,000 horse power) out-and-out two seat racing cars, individually built in ones and twos, which contested races such as Can-Am and the later years of Le Mans.

Bristol

Preserving the continuity of a design does not mean simply keeping it the same. Even Morgan had to make concessions to change when certain engines or components were no longer available. Some changes at Bristol came about through necessity but more often they were evolutionary. Either way, they were carried out with the same sort of meticulousness and care that distinguished the Rolls-Royce school of engineering philosophy. Bristol were never daunted by complication, believing that given sufficient care in its construction, nothing is too much trouble.

After the war, the Bristol Aeroplane Company of Filton near Bristol felt it necessary to diversify into car manufacture. Amongst the designs tried and abandoned was one by the chief engineer, Sir Roy Fedden, for a car with independent suspension and a sleeve-valve radial engine at the back. The idea of a more conventional, high-quality sporting saloon came later, through H. J. Aldington of AFN Ltd, who had imported BMWs before the war, selling them in Britain as Frazer Nash BMWs.

Aldington was a director of Bristol, and lost no time in renewing contact with the shattered remnants of the old Bayerische Motoren Werke, the greater part of which was now in the Russian-occupied zone. Aldington helped secure the release of BMW's former chief designer, and through the War Reparations Board obtained the design rights for the splendid range of cars BMW had been making in the Thirties.

Amongst these was the BMW 328, one of the most infuential sports car designs of modern times in both its production form, and the lightweight racing version which won the 1940 Mille Miglia (see page 25). The first Bristol, the Type 400, took some of the best features of the range, including the notable six cylinder engine with its ingenious cross-pushrod arrangement, adapted from an earlier design to provide a classic inclined-valve head. Its downdraught inlet tracts resulted in the characteristically tall engine which proved such an installation problem when it was subsequently used in the AC Ace, Frazer Nash, and Cooper-Bristol single-seat racing car.

The engine was refined and developed, producing 80 bhp at 4,200 rpm in the 1947 Bristol, and later over 130 bhp at 5,500 rpm in more sporting cars such as the Arnolt Bristol produced for the United States by 'Wacky' Arnolt through his connections with Bertone. Racing versions, such as used in the Le Mans Bristols which ran with impressive regularity in 1953-54, gave up to 160 bhp, while some Cooper-Bristols of the sort in which Mike Hawthorn established his reputation gave over 170 bhp, though at the expense of some reliability.

The Bristols types 400 to 406, produced from 1946 to 1961, all had this astonishing engine. All Bristols had a chassis built up on box-section frames which over the years changed in detail and underwent suspension alterations, but it preserved its essential characteristics of strength and safety throughout. Bristols may be said to have matured as their owners grew older — but that did not mean they became any slower. Though ever more luxurious and better finished, they remained amongst the fastest four-seat cars made in the world.

The voluptuously curvaceous 400 had outstanding handling and light steering; qualities which gave it the best competition record of any Bristol, except the 450. It was still produced alongside the 401, introduced in 1948 with the more fashionable 'Superleggera' bodywork, but the handling began to deteriorate, and the cars became less sporting until the introduction of the most-admired Bristol ever, the 404. The smallest Bristol made, on the same short 96¼in wheelbase as the lightweight, rather spartan Arnolt-Bristols, the 404 is also one of the rarest, only 40 ever being built with an elegant two-door body and tiny fins at the back. With 125 bhp and a better gearchange, the 404 evolved into the four door 405, whose wood-framed body has bedevilled restorers ever since. This was followed in 1958 by the milder-mannered 406 which was costlier, roomier and angled towards the Bentley market.

The repercussions of the De Havilland Comet accidents were felt throughout the aircraft industry. Cash had to be diverted to research and development on the aeroplane side of Bristol, causing the abandonment of a new model programme of great promise. Rival engines of greater power and flexibility left the 2 litre six-cylinder Bristol behind, and bereft of the twin ohc 3.65 litre replacement which had been designed by Stewart Tresilian, the firm had to look elsewhere.

Historic line-up of Bristol cars. From the right; Cooper-Bristol offset single seater Formula 1/2 car; 1955 Type 450 class-winning Le Mans car; original Type 400, built from 1947; Type 401 1949-53; rare 402 drophead; 404 coupe; 405 saloon; 406/407, last Bristol/first Chrysler engined car; 408/409; 410 and Beaufighter. Identification features which show the first of the two cars at the back to be a 407 include the body moulding and nave plates; the rear one is a square-radiatored 408.

There had been a tradition in Britain of looking to America for big, lusty engines, and Bristol commissioned a special version of the 5.1 litre Chrysler V-8 for the Type 407 introduced in 1961. Employing automatic transmission and a relatively slow-revving engine, the 407 was the very antithesis of its highly-tuned, high-revving predecessors, which required constant gear changing for maximum performance. The entire character of the Bristol car changed. Strong acceleration and a top speed of 120 mph brought it into a high-performance luxury league. The 408 of 1966 was a restyled version of the same car (if 'styling' is a word which can be applied to Bristols) and had the welcome addition of ZF power steering to meet the

criticism that too much muscular effort was required at parking speeds.

Bristol were now in a market for exclusive cars having all the traditional qualities of a Rolls-Royce. The difference was that they offered very high performance and lacked ostentation. They continued to be built with fine coachwork and all the engineering care of the aircraft industry, even though the Car Division had been hived off in 1966 on the merger between Bristol Siddeley and Rolls-Royce Aero Engines. For eighteen years production had been 150 cars a year, and that was where it remained with the fastest Bristol ever, carrying the name of a famous aeroplane, the Beaufighter. This 5.9 litre, 140 mph car took the firm into the turbocharged era.

At the rear, the supremely elegant Bristol 404 coupé, whose tiny rear fins echoed the contemporary Pegaso. Styling was usually left to others such as Zagato, who made the bodies for this 1959 version of the 406, of which only six were made.

A lower roof line and slimmer, less wrap-round windscreen pillars distinguished the Facel II, which looked less massive — almost slender — compared with the HK 500. This 1964 model also had the re-styled front, which was a good deal neater without sacrificing the car's imposing appearance.

Facel Vega

Forges et Ateliers de Construction d'Eure et de Loire, or FACEL, made bodies for Panhard, Simca, and Ford as well as engineering items ranging from kitchen equipment to gas turbine components. When Panhard decided to go elsewhere, the works at Colombes was left with spare capacity, and went ahead to build cars on its own account. Large, impressive, beautifully finished, with tuned Chrysler V-8 engines and the option of an all-synchromesh Pont-à-Mousson manual gearbox or a push-button Chrysler automatic transmission, the exclusive Vegas constituted France's most convincing bid for the luxury GT market.

Unfortunately, the market was small, and there proved to be not enough customers to go round. Facel offered the world excellence which it could not afford.

The first model was announced in 1954 with a 4½ litre, 180 bhp engine installed in the customary tubular frame to which the bodies were welded. Subsequent models went up to 5.8 litres and 325 bhp, and ultimately to 390 bhp with the big 6¼ litre, giving this massive car with its rather precipitous front a top speed of over 130 mph. Inside, the facia was covered in figured walnut, and the impressive array of instruments resembled those of an aircraft.

The Facel was by no means old-fashioned, yet it did preserve the ancient principle that anyone who wanted to make a faster car than the next man only had to apply more and more power, and he need no longer concern himself with the weight of the luxury, the sound-damping, or the elegance that he carried around. The Facel II weighed the best part of 2 tons on the road and measured nearly 15 ft 6in from its impressive prow to its shapely stern. Power steering, servo assisted brakes and electric windows gave the car a combination of ease of driving and speed which set it, in most respects, well ahead of its time. By 1980 keen drivers may have thought such refinement as the Facel offered in 1960 commonplace, but it was won expensively. It cost half as much again as the top Mercedes-Benz in Britain, and consumed fuel at a rate of some 14 mpg (20.2 litres/100 km).

Yet it was not this lively leviathan that brought about Facel's downfall. The firm's principal, Jean Daninos, felt there was room in the market for something smaller to complement his flagships. Accordingly, in 1958 he embarked on the design of a new, small, quality car, which he called the Facellia. Pont-à-Mousson, who already made the Facel transmission, commissioned Carlo Marchetti, formerly of Talbot, to produce a 1.6 litre twin overhead camshaft four cylinder engine. It turned out 115 bhp at 6,400 rpm — a high speed for the late

Fifties, demanding construction and assembly of the very highest quality and precision.

Unfortunately, the powerful little engine suffered from persistent piston failures, and by 1963 Daninos, in some desperation, turned to Volvo for P 1800 power units. The Facellia became the Facel III, slower than the Facellia but more reliable. In an effort to regain the performance market yet another version, powered by an Austin-Healey 3000 six cylinder engine, was planned, but only a few were made. Fresh capital was acquired from Pont-à-Mousson, Hisp-ano-Suiza, and Mobil-France; new management was appointed — but it was too late. By the beginning of 1965, the firm had closed down.

Somehow, the market for large luxury GT cars was always being over-estimated. The moment the 1973 fuel crisis struck, a number of manufacturers making large, American-engined, thirsty cars began to feel the pinch. Only those making cars with unusually convincing antecedents would survive. As for the handful making their own engines, such as Ferrari, even they needed a convincing racing pedigree to pull through. Had Facel struggled through this crisis, they might have been able to diversify into other products, or sell their services as consultants like Lotus or Porsche, but cars such as the Vega would probably not have seen the crisis-laden Seventies through.

Perhaps it was just as well that they left the scene when they did, remembered for their excellence; power-assisted pioneers, able to shink vast dimensions into manageable proportions on the road.

Ferrari

The influence of Enzo Ferrari on the sporting car has been incalculable. More than Ettore Bugatti in promoting it as an art form, more than Colin Chap-man whose technical contribution to automotive engineering was almost certainly more profound, more even than the technical genius of Dr Porsche — Ferrari epitomized the emotional approach to the sports car.

No-one had such a long, continuous-ly active relationship with the topmost levels of motor racing. As a driver for Alfa Romeo in the Twenties, as founder of the Scuderia Ferrari in 1929, as a constructor just before the war, then as the manufacturer of what became the archetypal sporting car, Ferrari influ-enced an entire generation. His cars were more than a motoring *haute couture:* they became badges of wealth

Pininfarina's long-standing relationship with Ferrari dated from 1952, the year of this 212 Inter, with rather heavy frontal aspect but well-sculpted profile. By 1967, however, he was getting the hang of it, as witness the sweeping lines of this 330 GTC.

Coupe with four cams, the Ferrari 275 GTB4 of 1967 (identify the GTB4 from other GTBs by the slight bulge in the bonnet top) took some of the best styling features of the famous GTO to create one of the great road-going Ferraris. Yet it was not an easy car to see out of, and the pierced disc wheels replacing the traditional Borrani wire wheels were regarded as aesthetically retrograde at the time. Jean-Pierre Beltoise described it in *l'Auto Journal* as, 'One of the greatest automobiles created in our times'.

for the rich and ennobled, the guinea-stamp of rank throughout the Western world.

The Scuderia Ferrari was a commercial stable set up by the former racing driver to breed new strains of racing cars. Hired by Alfa Romeo, it was subsequently fired when it failed to beat the Germans' technical overkill in the Grand Prix racing of the Thirties. Worse still was a legal sanction preventing Ferrari making cars of his own for two years — a safeguard against using Alfa Romeo know-how to beat them at their own game.

By entering under the banner of Auto Avio Costruzione, Ferrari's machine tool firm, the first surrogate Ferraris took part in the 1940 Brescia Grand Prix (the 1940 Mille Miglia), one of them driven by Alberto Ascari, whose father Antonio had been an old colleague of Ferrari's. Hurriedly made from Fiat components, the cars were relatively undistinguished, yet they were the ancestors of an entire dynasty of aristocrats.

In a Europe racked by war, recovery was slow. Petrol was in short supply, resources for essential transport scarce. Building sports cars of any sort was an act of either faith or folly. Building one with a V-12 engine and the performance of a racing car appeared extravagant and reckless.

The reason for using a twelve cylinder engine was partly technical, but mostly emotive. The appeal of the machinery was enhanced by the beauty of the bodies created by Carrozzeria Bertone, 'Superleggera' Touring, Scaglietti, Allemano, Ghia, Zagato, Vignale, and above all, Pinin Farina. Their sense of style was matchless, their proportions almost always elegant. The rich and famous beat a path to the door of Ferrari's tiny factory at Maranello near Modena, traditional home of the Italian sports car.

As *'Le Pur Sang des Automobiles'*, Ferrari probably took over where Bugatti left off, but that does not mean the road cars were beyond reproach. The dictum that today's racing cars are tomorrow's sports cars was never followed so closely. The first model with the Gioacchino Colombo V-12, the Type 125, was sold in three forms: Sport, Competizione, and Gran Premio. It was really much the same car fitted respectively with (a) stylish two-seat open bodywork (b) lightweight open two-seat 'Barchetta' body with cycle-type wings and lights, and (c) single-seat racing body.

With few exceptions, Ferrari's type numbers, until the later years of the flat-twelves, were based on the capacity of the individual cylinders. The 125

All a driver wants to know. Immediately behind the wheel, the big dials are speed in km/h on the left, and rev counter (tachometer) on the right, red-lined at 6,500. Top small gauge is oil pressure, lower engine temperature. Four dials angled towards the driver are a clock, fuel gauge, oil temperature, and ammeter. The car, a luxury 1976 Ferrari 400 automatic.

engine dimensions were 55mm bore x 52.5mm stroke, making 1,466.77cc, one-twelfth of which was close enough to 125 to give the model a designation. When Aurelio Lampredi enlarged it, it became the 166, and with a twin cam head per bank it became progressively bigger as the 195 and 212 Inter, the 340 America, 250 Export, 225 Sport, 250 GT, and ultimately the 375 4½ litre GP of 1954.

The performance was always staggering. The handling and roadholding on the other hand were at best variable; the gearboxes were generally difficult, with indifferent synchromesh — when it was provided at all. The one-off road cars often had bodywork that was rudimentary, in pursuit of lightness, for the goal was always performance. Ferrari's days as a builder of luxury sports cars came later.

Between 1949 and 1954 the little factory produced only 200 road cars; only 35 were made throughout 1954 compared with around 250 sports-racing or competition Ferraris, excluding single-seaters. But with the

overleaf
Short wheelbase Berlinetta, the 250GT by Scaglietti was available in both steel and alloy. In racing trim it succeeded the 250GT Tour de France, and was the precursor of the great classic coupe, the superb GTO.

The production, 'cleaned-up' Ferrari 500 Superfast by Pininfarina. Prototypes from 1960 suffered from mouldings along the body sides, and bonnet air intakes, but the smoothed-off production model, of which only around 30 were ever made, turned out to be one of the most supremely elegant Ferraris.

Rare Ferrari. The 365 California, of which only about 13 were ever made, in 1966 and 1967, effectively replaced the 500 Superfast. This is the Pininfarina prototype shown at the 1966 Geneva Salon, with a very angular rear contrasting with the soft curves at the front.

introduction of the 250 GT things changed. This was the first model to be built in anything approaching series production, and by 1964 was being turned out at the rate of 670 per year, mostly with bodies made by Pininfarina (no longer double-barrelled) who came close to being Ferrari's exclusive body supplier.

The 4 cylinder engine introduced for the 1950-51 season seemed the very antithesis of the howling, high-revving V-12s, but as racing power plants they displayed unparallelled efficiency. Lighter, simpler, with fewer parts and lower friction losses than the twelves, they overwhelmed the opposition in Formula 2 Grand Prix racing in 1952-53, and founded a line of sports cars which included the 2 litre 170 bhp Type 500 Mondial. A later version became the first Testa Rossa.

Up to the advent of the luxury versions of the 250 GT and later more refined models, driving a Ferrari was like driving a racing car. Mechanical clatter from the valve gear and the whine of straight-cut racing gears were considered the concomitant of speed. The handling needed to be taut and nervous, the ride firm. The Ferrari was to be driven decisively; a car to be taken seriously because it was very, very fast.

The ancestor of the Dino, named after Ferrari's son who died young, and over whom his father grieved for the rest of his life, was the Lancia D 50 V-8. Ferrari inherited the Lancia racing team in 1956, and Vittorio Jano based his ingenious V-6 on its 4 ohc heads. It was an engine on which changes were endlessly rung, with the cylinders at 65° and 120°, and with 2, 3 and 4 valves per

cylinder. Besides powering the production range of mid-engined Dino sports cars, it also found its way back into a Lancia, the Stratos rally car of the Seventies.

Yet the most spectacular Ferrari of all was still to come. Faced with the problem of getting the centre of gravity on the Formula 1 racing cars even lower, chief engineer Mauro Forghieri took the rather tall Type 312 V-12 and effectively laid the cylinders out flat. The 312B, for *Boxermotor*, became the basis of the

Racing connections. Unveiled at the 1975 Paris Motor Show, the 308 GTB Ferrari used a V-8 engine behind the driver. Early examples had plastic bodies.

flat-twelve road cars, duly carrying on the racing car to sports car tradition so faithfully preserved by Ferrari. The engines are not the same of course. The road car's has seven main bearings, the racing car's four. In the racing engines the delivery of the maximum power, with the customary between-races rebuilds, is all — while the road cars' requirements are for smoothness and longevity. Nevertheless, the road car is one of the fastest production machines in the world, capable of more than 180 mph.

The launch of the Berlinetta Boxer coincided with Ferrari's Grand Prix comeback of the Seventies, when Niki Lauda won two brilliant world championships, narrowly and tragically missing a third. It copied the racing car's ground-hugging aerodynamics and superb balance, giving the driver not only the straight line speed for which Ferraris have always been renowned, but also the astonishing road grip enabled by the adoption of the mid-engined configuration.

Dry-sump lubrication; rear wheels increased to 9 inches wide; front spoiler; 360 horse power, the 5 litre 512 Berlinetta Boxer flat-12 revived memories of the sport racing cars of only five years earlier when it appeared at the Paris Salon as a road car in 1976.

Ford GT 40

By 1963, the mid-engined concept for sports racing cars was well established. Yet most of them were still open cars, and it seemed only a matter of time before the inherent advantages of a closed car (deeper-section frame with the strengthening effect of a roof, better aerodynamics, etc.,) would result in a mid-engined coupe.

At Bromley in South East London, Eric Broadley, already a successful designer of a wide range of racing cars, was working on an idea, while far away in Detroit the giant Ford Motor Company was taking its first tentative steps towards becoming involved in motor racing. These steps took the tangible shape of the Mustang I.

This was not to be confused with later cars of the same name. Mustang I was a 1.7 litre mid-engined open two seater designed by Roy Lunn, an expatriate Englishman, as much to test public opinion for Ford's coming competitions effort as anything else. It was an interesting engineering exercise as well, but no more. It was not a GT 40 in embryo any more than Eric Broadley had intended his Lola GT to be.

Yet Broadley was nearer the mark for the car Ford had in mind. He introduced it at the London Racing Car Show in January 1963, where it proved to be amongst the star attractions. It certainly attracted the attention of the team Ford had assigned to get them into racing. They had already been rebuffed by Ferrari; now they saw in the Lola a short-cut, conceived by one of the best brains in racing, a short-cut they knew at once they had to take.

Ford Advanced Vehicles was formed, and the Lola was appraised, dismembered, amended, and developed. It was wind-tunnelled, and mocked-up. It was subjected to the sort of far-reaching programme of which only Americans, with their vast resources of men and material, are capable. It was the automotive equivalent of NASA's moon project.

Ford's objective was a little nearer to home. It was to win the 24 Hours race at Le Mans.

No other event in the world has so captured the motor racing imagination. Le Mans was where the first Grand Prix took place — not quite on the same circuit of roads, but close enough. Le Mans was where the Wright brothers first flew their aircraft in Europe (on 8 August, 1908, on the racecourse near Les Hunaudières). And Le Mans was where Ford decided they would take the world of motor racing by storm.

The chosen vehicle was the GT 40. No space probe was ever put together more carefully; no satellite researched so thoroughly. Nothing was too much trouble — or too expensive.

A pontoon-type monocoque hull was built up from 23-gauge sheet steel, and instead of the Lola's tubular sub-frames at the back and front, more sheet metal sections carried the front suspension pick-up points and the Ford 4.2 litre Indianapolis V-8. The rear suspension was carried by a similar structure at the back. The engine was ahead of the rear axle line, and although the weight distribution of the prototype cars had a heavy rearward bias (43:57), a better balance was achieved later.

The large sills contained fuel in bag tanks, and the outer skin was in panels of glass-reinforced plastic. The roof superstructure added to the beam stiffness, although the doors were carried up into the roof panel, leaving only a narrow spine in the centre. Detail items included an elaborate system of ducting air for driver cooling; the seat was fixed and the pedals and steering were adjustable.

As things turned out, the early cars were less than perfect. At the Le Mans test week-end in the Spring of 1964 Jo Schlesser, the French driver who was later to lose his life so tragically in the French Grand Prix at Rouen, became airborne at about 150 mph in the almost flat-out bend in the middle of the Mulsanne straight. In the bland NASA-style jargon of the day, Lunn confessed that '. . . some stability phenomenon existed that had not become apparent during the design analytical phase.' In other words the car was developing aerodynamic lift — after all it was doing the speeds at which fully-laden aircraft will cheerfully take off . . .

Ford did not win Le Mans in 1964.

They did not win in 1965 either, although they did win Daytona by way of compensation.

By 1966 the 7 litre Mark 2 was available, the team was reorganized, they won Daytona again, and with no fewer than eight cars in three teams, they won Le Mans at last. Bruce McLaren and Chris Amon gave Ford the victory they coveted, and which reputedly cost them 9 million dollars.

If anything, perhaps the greatest racing days of the cars were yet to come. They went up to Mark 4, and their construction became more and more exotic, with aluminium honeycomb sandwich panels, and ever more power and speed. They won at Sebring three times, they won the Spa 1000 Km twice, they won Le Mans again in 1967 (Gurney/Foyt), 1968 (Rodriguez/ Bianchi), and yet again in 1969 in the most dramatic finish ever, when Jacky Ickx beat the Porsche 917 of Hans Herrmann by a matter of yards. They won the Rheims 12 Hours, the Paris 1000 Km, the Kyalami 9 Hours twice, and the BOAC 500 at Brands Hatch — the list was seemingly endless.

Of the 107 GT 40s built, half a dozen were road cars, although over thirty were converted to road trim later. Apart from a certain amount of difficulty seeing out, especially rearwards, they could be made surprisingly easy to drive, and sufficiently docile to trickle along in traffic whilst retaining a great deal of performance. Like many sports racing cars, the ride of the GT 40 was good — it soaked up bumps in a most exemplary manner, although the suspension could make some alarming noises, and the ground clearance meant the driver had to be on the lookout for tall kerbs.

The most famous Ford? Perhaps. It became so much of a collector's item that JW Automotive, who retained the design rights when Ford withdrew from racing, began making a few more as the Eighties dawned — for very wealthy collectors who found their originals starting to wear out.

A dramatic road car, the GT 40 was principally a Le Mans racer in its various forms. It had to be de-tuned and tamed for road use, which had a chastening effect on its 200mph performance, but rendered it quite practical, if a little cramped, for cutting a dash on the highway. The two scoops in the bonnet top draw air through the front intake and past the water and oil radiators.

Frazer Nash

The last old-style Frazer Nash, complete with its primitive final drive by chains, was built in 1939. By then the Aldington family had been in control of the business founded by Archie Frazer Nash for ten years, and the astute arrangement by which AFN Ltd had become concessionaires for the excellent BMW cars in Britain was bearing a good deal of commercial fruit.

After the war, H. J. Aldington encouraged an accommodation between BMW and Bristol. He was a director of Bristol, so it was not surprising that when Frazer Nash went back to making cars they appeared with a special version of the BMW/Bristol 2 litre engine. The deal was for Bristol to make the engine and keep it for their touring cars, and for Frazer Nash to retain the right to use it for sports cars. It was a reasonable arrangement, and to further it, Aldington used his connections with BMW to persuade Dr Fiedler to come to England and work with Bristol.

The new Frazer Nash sports cars shared with Bristol the same transmission and much the same rear suspension. The independent front suspension, by a transverse leaf spring and lower wishbones, was based on the pre-war BMW 328; the rear had an A-bracket and longitudinal torsion bars.

The likeness to the 328 even extended to the pierced steel disc wheels with centre-lock fixing, but the chassis frame was made from rather larger diameter (5in) seamless steel tubes which were not, as reputedly on the 328, of varying thickness according to where the stresses fell.

Two new models made their appearance in 1948, one with full-width bodywork known as the Fast Roadster, and one in racing trim, with cycle-type wings and a rounded-off lightweight shell, called the High Speed Model. After Aldington and Norman Culpan had driven it to a creditable third place in the revived Le Mans 24 Hours race in 1949, it was called the Le Mans Replica, and was also available with single-seat bodywork for Formula 2 racing.

Sixty Le Mans Replicas were made — a long run by Frazer Nash standards. A Mark II version appeared in 1952 with a de Dion rear axle, like the somewhat more stylish Sebring model, but by then Frazer Nash, like many another minority manufacturer, was in the slipstream of Jaguar. The small bespoke specialist could not compete in the market place with the XK 120, which was setting the pace and catching the eye much as the 328 BMW had over a decade earlier.

In an effort to remain in contention, an alternative engine to the expensive Bristol was sought. A Roadster was offered in 1952 with an Austin Atlantic engine — unworthy of the marque, and in any case quickly overwhelmed by the arrival of the Austin-Healey. A prototype was made with an Armstrong-Siddeley engine, but it did no better. The Continental model was tried, using the new BMW V-8, but this too was destined for failure.

AFN carried on making a handful of cars to special order, but their Falcon Works at Isleworth near London was soon busy as the importing centre for another German car in the best radical tradition of the BMW 328. AFN Ltd took on the concession for Porsche and in due course made the United Kingdom the best export market for the make after the United States.

above
Third place in the first postwar Le Mans, 1949, earned the High Speed Model Frazer Nash the title Le Mans Replica. Cycle-type wings, sketchy bodywork and minimal weather protection were still regarded as normal for a true sports car.

left
Introduced in 1953, this Le Mans Frazer Nash was in effect a coupe version of the Sebring open two seater.

Jaguar

Few cars have been able to flavour modern British social history like the Jaguar has. As evocative as East End, stockbroker, or commuter, the so-called 'Gin and Jag' belt was a conception of *nouveau riches* as unfair to the car as to the people. The sneer, however, was something of a legacy. SS cars of the Thirties only became prized after Jaguar attained respectability. They were not highly regarded by sports car enthusiasts of the time. Generally considered cheap and shoddy, they were even advertised as 'The car with the £1,000 look', when they sold for £325.

Sir William, as plain Bill Lyons, was regarded as a motorcycle sidecar manufacturer trying to move up-market. He made flashy bodies for cars, to be sold by his chum, Bertie Henly. To the posh Brooklands crowd, the SS was a bit *infra dig*, with a long bonnet concealing a relatively small engine.

When Jaguar was revived after the war, therefore, it had somehow as much to live down as live up to. It seemed, to Lyons and his team of engineers, which included Claude Baily, Walter Hassan, and William Heynes, that the best means of publicizing the magnificent engine they were bringing out for their new saloons was to make a short production run, say 200, of a dramatic looking sports car. This could be raced a few times, gain a bit of a reputation, and then be put away again.

As for the engine, efficiency had demanded a twin overhead camshaft engine in the classic pattern, and after designing some and building others in the X (for experimental) series, they had come to the six cylinder XK. Installed in

the 'limited edition' batch of sports cars, estimated capable of 120 mph with aluminium bodywork, it became the powerhouse of the great XK 120. The team had been admirers of the BMW 328, and the styling was based on the 1940 Mille Miglia cars, although altogether sleeker and better proportioned.

When the XK appeared at the Earls Court Motor Show in October 1948, the response was immediate. There was nothing for it but to tool up, build the car with a steel body, and get it into production alongside the superb Mark VIII saloon.

After proving it could do 130 mph without the aerodynamic drawback of a windscreen, the XK went racing. It suffered from overheating brakes — a result of the immense performance with the shrouding effect of the bodywork and steel disc wheels. Yet it acquitted

itself well, earning its spurs as a sports car in the best sense of the term, and not just as something to catch the eye on the promenade.

Yet it was not until the advent of the XK 120C (for Competition) version that the racing world took the car seriously. A tubular frame, rear axle location by A-bracket, torque arm and Panhard rod, and the C-Type, as it was soon called, romped home to victory at Le Mans in 1951, driven by Peter Walker and Peter Whitehead. With the new disc brakes it won again in 1953 (Duncan Hamilton/ Tony Rolt), narrowly missing a convincing 1-2-3.

The 1954 Jaguar, beaten by a Ferrari 375 by a matter of two miles (the fourth-closest margin in the history of the race) was known, following the C, as the D-Type. One of the all-time greats amongst sporting cars, the D-Type won Le Mans in 1955 (Mike Hawthorn/Ivor

The superb profile of the E-Type in its purest Mark 1 form, with the fully faired-in headlights (later altered because of upward light scatter) and slim bumpers. From its introduction in 1961, the E-Type became the benchmark in speed, style and handling for an entire generation of sports cars.

above
Jaguar C-Types fill the leading positions on the front row of the grid at Mallory Park on 6 July, 1957. Their rivals include Austin-Healey 100S, Lotus XI, AC, and XK 120.

right
Ivor Bueb at the wheel of the 1957 Le Mans winning D-Type Jaguar he shared with Ron Flockhart. This was the second time the Scottish team of Ecurie Ecosse won the 24- Hour classic.

Bueb), 1956 (Ninian Sanderson/Ron Flockhart), and 1957 (Flockhart/Bueb, a second triumph for Ecurie Ecosse). Only Ferrari, with nine victories in thirty years, beat Jaguar's five: only Bentley, Jaguar, Alfa Romeo and Ferrari ever won the race four years in a row, and in 1957 Jaguar gained the most overwhelming Le Mans victory ever. In a unique performance, five Jaguars started and five finished, first, second, third, fourth, and sixth.

The D-Type was every inch a sports racer, from its graceful, well-rounded nose (longer on the later cars) to the tip of its famous tail fin. It could do 185 mph down Mulsanne, yet it was an unexpectedly easy car to drive. This was an era of heavy, multi-plate racing clutches, muscular steering, and engines with power curves which tended to peak at high revs but offered little low down, making progress at anything but racing speeds jerky and problematical. The D-Type, on the other hand, could be driven on the the road — it often was. In his

amateur days, Jim Clark used to drive the Border Reivers' D-Type to race meetings in Scotland and the North of England.

Far from being 'one-off' racing cars, D-Types were actually made on a production line. In all, there were 71 of them, and the factory in Coventry was about to start making its successor in quantity, the XKSS, when a disastrous fire threw the entire Jaguar sports car programme into disarray.

The XK had become the 140, then the 150, with changes which were largely cosmetic. They remained essentially cars in which the occupants sat atop a deep box-section frame braced with a pressed steel cruciform. It was old fashioned when the car was rushed into production in 1949; by 1959 it was looking rather unworthy of the thoroughly advanced XK engine, but then the monocoque XKSS should have replaced it. However, it had paid its way. Far from being a small series of cars produced for publicity purposes, more than 12,000

XK 120s, 9,000 XK 140s, and 9,400 XK 150s were sold. The range included open two seaters, coupes, and two-plus-twos, that apologetic euphemism applied to cars when the back seats are described as 'occasional', or 'restricted', when what is really meant is 'small', or 'impractical'.

The XK was no match for the modern, low, space-framed sports cars, which had less body roll, less weight, and a lower centre of gravity. The Jaguars, with their tall, narrow tyres and heavy gearchanges, were relegated to the role of dignified tourers, rather than the *avant garde* sporting machines they had been in 1949.

Even if the XKSS represented a sort of lost generation of Jaguar sports cars through its unfortunate still-birth, the E-Type when it came in 1961 was still a striking descendant. It shared with the BMW 328 the distinction of being the yardstick by which almost every other sports car would come to be judged. It was breathtakingly beautiful and its

left
Still a clear relation of the XK 120, the 150 was more mature, and displayed a certain amount of middle-age spread. Bumpers and chrome strips did little for the graceful lines. Discreet S motif on the door signifies three 2-in SU carburettors giving 250bhp instead of the normal 210.

below
Bearing a clear resemblance to the racing D-Type, the Jaguar XKSS was the road-going production version until the fire in the factory in 1957.

Lamborghini

E2A, the sports prototype which would have replaced the D-Type, and turned out to be the precursor of the E-Type instead. In Briggs Cunningham's American racing colours it took part in the 1960 Le Mans, but failed to finish.

road manners were faultless. It rode bumps like a limousine and it handled with consummate precision and safety; as a road-going sports car its performance was unparalleled, and its steering and cornering power were matchless. In addition, like all Jaguars before it, produced in a factory where costs were watched with almost puritanical parsimony, it cost about one-third of the price of the equivalent Ferrari.

Of course, Jaguars never had the longevity of many of the other Grand Marques — enthusiasts who restore them fight a never ending campaign against rust. But for sheer value they were never matched.

Even when the V-12 versions came on the scene in 1971, just in time to suffer from the effects of the oil crisis with their fuel consumption of around 15-17 mpg, they were highly competitive in the market place. Similarly, the XJS, although rather less of a real sports car than the E-Type, was always a lot of car for the money.

Jaguar's place in the overall scheme of things has been important. In certain aspects of design, notably the D-Type independent rear suspension, and the XK engine, they were technically sophisticated. In others, such as gearboxes and auxiliary equipment such as heaters (*heaters? in sports cars?*) they remained in the automotive dark ages. Yet they were such successful packages, such great combinations of virtues, that they drove into eclipse many other fine makers of sports cars who failed to realize their commercial possibilities.

The XK 120, the D-Type and the E-Type remain amongst the highest summits of sports car attainment.

Not many great cars have been created by committees. The Ford GT 40 perhaps, or some latter-day Lancias or Mercedes-Benz. Most of the Grand Marques were influenced by individuals — Sir William Lyons, Colin Chapman, Ettore Bugatti, Enzo Ferrari — either in their style or in their technicalities, or just simply in the way they were conceived.

Ferrucio Lamborghini was one such visionary.

After a successful career making air conditioning equipment and air-cooled diesel tractors, which occupied an important place in the Italian market

behind Fiat and Massey-Ferguson, Lamborghini put his money and his passion into cars. He had been obsessed with them all his life, to the extent of competing in the 1948 Mille Miglia. He had an antipathy to Ferraris ever since he got a dusty answer, like so many customers, from the old man of Maranello when something had gone wrong with one.

Lamborghinis, he decided, would be the best sports and GT cars in the world.

He recruited with care. He was still only 45 in 1961, when he founded Automobili Ferrucio Lamborghini at Sant'Agata Bolognese. His engine man was 36-year-old Giotto Bizzarini, one of the engineers who had just defected from Ferrari, along with Ing. Chiti,

Romolo Tavoni, and Phil Hill. Bizzarini had been developing the famous Ferrari GTO, and Lamborghini set him designing another V-12, with four overhead camshafts, capable of high speed and power, and with dry sump lubrication for racing.

The chassis was to be the work of 24-year-old Gianpaolo Dallara, a brilliant graduate of Milan Technical Institute. He too had worked with Chiti at Ferrari, and also with a cousin who would figure later in the Lamborghini story, Giulio Alfieri, who had been responsible for the most famous Maserati ever, the 250F, as well as the 'Birdcage' sports racing car. From Maserati, Lamborghini tempted Bob Wallace, a skilled New Zealander who

Photographed by the author at the new factory in May 1965, before even the road to the front office had been surfaced, one of the first 350GT Lamborghinis to be built. Essentially a two-seater, the 350GT was replaced in 1966 by the 400GT 2+2 with extra space within the Touring body, and a 4 litre engine.

would be test driver and development engineer.

This team produced the first 3½ litre Lamborghini, a conventional front-engined roadster of impeccable workmanship. Alas, the racing potential of that first engine was never to be realized. Shortly after it showed an encouraging 360 bhp on the test bench, Lamborghini turned his back on competition, for ever as it turned out, and had it de-tuned for smoothness and longevity instead. The result was a silken, turbine-like engine which gave the later 4 litre model a top speed of over 150 mph in astonishing silence.

The body was by Bertone, anxious to find a role like that of Pininfarina at Ferrari. Yet the car was built almost wholly 'in house' at Lamborghini's elegant new factory, brimming with fine machinery and producing the hand-finished supercars that were to establish the new firm amongst the classics.

The first cars, however, were less than perfect. The single wiper lifted off the screen at even moderate speed, and the gear ratios were peculiar, with

The chisel nose and the fold-flat headlights made the Lamborghini Miura look every inch a Le Mans racer. Yet the makers made a point of avoiding involvement with competition, even by proxy.

65 mph available in first, and only 85 in second. But the foundations of a reputation for exquisite engineering had been laid.

It was with his next car that Lamborghini was to become best known. By the mid-Sixties, the mid-engined concept was gaining ground as the ideal layout for excellence in balance and road holding. The single seater world had gone over to it entirely, and the Ford GT 40 had shown the way for the creation of a mid-engined coupe. Yet finding the space for a long V-12, as opposed to a more compact V-8, would provide engineers something of a

challenge. How could they find the space within the compass of a practical mid-engined road car?

Dallara, his assistant Paolo Stanzani, and Bob Wallace worked out an elegant solution. In 1956 Bugatti had fielded a short-lived Grand Prix car, the Type 251. Unlike almost anything else Bugatti ever did, its design was years ahead of its time, with an eight cylinder engine mounted transversely in the frame just behind the driver.

As a Grand Prix car it was less than a success, but Dallara seized on its example as a solution to his problem of shoe-horning his big V-12. With engine

block, crankcase and transmission combined in one extremely complicated alloy casting, he produced the fabulous Miura. He completed his masterpiece with a platform chassis of sheet steel with box-section cross members, and box section sills and backbone. It was the very antithesis of the customary Modenese *tubolare*; it exemplified Italian metalworking artistry with all the fine proportion and curvilineal grace that implies, as convincingly as the GT 40 demonstrated the supreme technology of the Americans.

The result in both cases was a car of style and pace. Lamborghini showed the Miura at the Turin Show in 1965, still in chassis form, catching the imagination of the Italian coachbuiders, but arousing the suspicions of engineers, who sensed the car was still at an early stage of its development. In truth, Lamborghini never expected to sell more than a handful, but by the time Bertone had clothed it in a body of dramatic beauty, there was no going back. Styled in the initial stages by Giorgetto Giugiaro, about to leave the position of Bertone's chief designer en route to setting up Ital Design, the Miura was the culmination of a process by which the sports car had so outstripped the mass-transport road car as to be almost unrecognizable.

The sacrifices in living-space remained, but otherwise it was as

above
In a sense the Jarama was a 2+2 version of the four-seat Espada; said to be Ferrucio Lamborghini's favourite, it was available from 1974 with Chrysler automatic transmission.

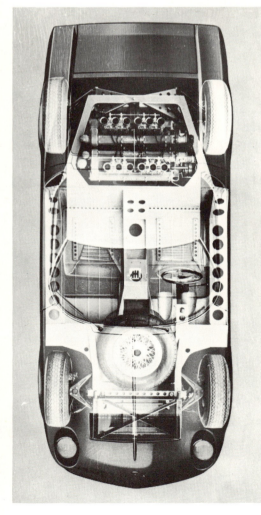

left
Its big V-12 mounted transversely, Bugatti-style, the Lamborghini Miura was one of the first mid-engined road-going coupes.

Influenced by the Marzal, an elaborately-windowed dream car with gullwing doors by Bertone, the Espada was the roomiest Lamborghini, and boasted four full-sized seats.

luxurious, as well-furnished, as refined, and rode as smoothly as the highest quality of upright limousine. Unlike many mid-engined designs such as the under-developed AC, it handled superbly, with no unmannerly surprises, even for novice drivers, beyond a first gear top speed close to 60 mph, second 85 mph, third 120 mph, fourth well over 150 mph, and fifth upwards of 170 mph, or more if there was room.

Since the engine air intakes were a matter of inches behind the driver's head, the Miura was a good deal less quiet than the original 250 and 400 GT, but it was the surging, exciting noise of a high-efficiency engine, so dear to the enthusiast's heart. Furthermore, the mid-engine position gave a taste of the low-slung, hammock style of driving seat in which the occupant reclined, after the fashion of the Grand Prix aces, by now it seemed almost lying down in an effort to reduce frontal area and keep the weight of the car near the ground.

The Miura was replaced by the Countach in 1971, but the front-engined Lamborghini lived on as the Espada and Jarama. Their continuing disregard for

racing made Lamborghini at pains to point out that the Jarama they meant was not the Spanish race track, but the town where fighting bulls were bred — Lamborghini names and badges featured bulls.

The Urraco was a transverse 2½ litre water-cooled V-8 with single overhead camshafts driven by toothed belts and was aimed clearly at the Ferrari Dino market. The suspension was by Mac-Pherson struts front and rear, a favourite of Dallara's. Alas, the more modest Lamborghinis were not modest enough. Like many another worthy supplier of sports cars to the nobility and gentry of the Western world, Lamborghini suffered agonies from the rising price of oil and the world recession which followed.

Production languished, then ceased. Ownership of the firm changed with first Swiss, then German cash until it went into receivership. Rescue was effected by Nuova Automobili Lamborghini which installed Giulio Alfieri, never far from the scene at Sant'Agata, to get things moving as the make approached the twentieth anniversary of its foundation.

Lancia

Vincenzo Lancia was a motor racing pioneer and an innovative engineer, yet he strenuously avoided putting his cars to the test of competition. In contrast to Alfa Romeo for example, he never entered a works team in races or rallies despite the advanced nature of designs such as the V-4 Lambda, with its unitary construction, independent front suspension, hydraulic dampers and four wheel brakes. This was 1922, and as we have seen, it was a prophetic conception of how sports cars would develop.

Lancia died in 1937 just as his last great car, the Aprilia, came out, with torsion bar suspension, a beautifully streamlined body, hypoid rear axle, and the unusual V-4 engine. It was a technical triumph that advanced the small car by a generation, and meant that whilst most other makes had perforce to take up somewhat antiquated designs when they resumed after the war, Lancia had an advanced philosophy ready and waiting.

Nonetheless, when Gianni Lancia took over from his father, he wanted something new. He engaged Vittorio Jano, formerly of Alfa Romeo, who kept the basic hull and suspension of the older Lancias, but the V-4 became a pushrod V-6, and the gearbox mounted on the rear axle gained synchromesh. Suspension was all independent and the rear brakes were inboard — it was a car with a specification made for racing, and that indeed was what Gianni wanted.

The Lancia company was conservative enough to remain dubious about a change in policy towards competition, but Gianni was adamant. Conditions, he argued, had changed since his father was alive, and racing was necessary to publicize a low-volume, superbly engineered GT car selling at something of a premium. In the event, racing was financially ruinous, and the Lancia family lost control of the firm which bore their name, but not before it had made some of the most desirable cars of the Fifties. The flag which was the emblem of one of Italy's best cars went down flying.

The convertible was the most popular of the 1962 Touring-bodied Lancia Flaminias. Looking like the GT Coupe, it is seen here with the factory hardtop; both models had the option of 2.5 or 2.8 litre engines.

Fifties favourite. The GT version of Lancia's Aurelia was one of the best-handling cars of the early Fifties. The two door 'fastback' style echoed Pininfarina's famous Cisitalia, and became the pattern for many GT cars to come.

The deeply wrapped-round windscreen of the 1952 B24 served to persuade the American market that Lancia were abreast of fashion. Less practical was the replacement of bumpers with nothing more than upright over-riders.

Jano's V-6 Aurelia was a landmark in design as much for its two door fastback body as anything else. It followed Pininfarina's Cisitalia form with a traditional Lancia heart-shaped grille. To meet the fashion of the moment it had a curious anomaly for a sports car: a steering column gearchange, without which, it was imagined, nobody in America would buy it. Yet by virtue of its equable weight distribution and independent suspension it was one of the best-handling road cars of the decade.

Encouraged by the Aurelia's victories in the 1953 Targa Florio, a class win at Le Mans, a second in the Mille Miglia and victories in the Liège-Rome-Liège and Monte Carlo Rallies, Gianni decided to go for an out-and-out sports racing car. The V-6 was redesigned with overhead cams, enlarged to 3 litres, and put into a space-framed open two seater. The independent suspension followed Jano's old Alfa style by having transverse leaf springs, but amongst the novel features were inboard brakes at the front as well as the back in an effort to reduce the unsprung weight imposed by the large drums. On some models the driver was given control over the

friction-type shock absorbers so that he could make the damping softer or harder.

Known as the D 20, the car had a variable career in competition until the 3.3 litre D 24 was developed. A de Dion rear axle, longer wheelbase, and more power made all the difference, and Lancia scored a resounding 1-2-3 in the epic Carrera Panamericana of 1953.

Undeterred by the rising costs of racing, Lancia embarked on a Grand Prix programme for 1954 whilst still racing the sports cars. Alberto Ascari won the Mille Miglia, narrowly losing the world sports car championship to Ferrari when the latest 3.8 litre D 24s, the brakes now mounted outboard for better cooling, failed in the decisive round, the Dundrod TT.

The financial writing, however, was on the wall. The D 24s never raced again; the Formula 1 project was handed over to Ferrari, and by 1956 Gianni Lancia had resigned. His gamble with motor racing was over and the Pesenti family took charge.

Although racing was considered imprudent, Lancia remained in rallying with the smaller, sprightlier cars in their rapidly ageing range. Professor Antonio Fessio was now technical director and, although working within tighter financial constraints than his immediate predecessors, he kept alive Lancia's tradition of radicalism by using the Appia's V-4 engine in the little Fulvia. This was a small front wheel drive car which appeared from 1965 as a neat, stylish Lancia-made coupe and an unhandsome but efficient-looking Zagato which would do 110 mph on 1,300cc.

But even the Pesenti money was not enough to keep Lancia building small, high quality sports cars, and by 1969 Fiat had to come to the rescue. It was well timed. Fiat were able to revive the competition programme with the Fulvia engine enlarged to 1.6 litres, giving 115 bhp, and win the Monte Carlo Rally and the world rally championship in 1972. They won the RAC Rally of Great Britain, regarded as one of the world's toughest events, twice, and through

below
Second thoughts proved better with the Mark 2 version of the Lancia Montecarlo, the mid-engined version of the Beta, and big brother to the Fiat X1/9.

bottom
January 1976, and Lancia win the Monte Carlo Rally with the mid-engined Stratos. Sandro Munari scored a total of four Monte victories with Lancia.

their connection with Ferrari, Fiat also supplied a Dino engine for the Lancia Stratos. This began life as a Bertone-inspired styling exercise in 1972.

The futuristic-looking Stratos became one of the most striking rally cars ever. To enthusiasts the world over it made Fiat's expensive takeover seem worthwhile, and it must have been worthwhile for Fiat too, giving them a prestige name in the sporting field.

Fiat gave Lancia a surprising amount of engineering autonomy. Lancias never became merely 'badge-engineered' Fiats although they used a certain amount of Fiat production mechanical parts, and the Beta and Gamma developed engineering characteristics entirely their own. The front-wheel-drive Beta was competitively priced against large-volume rivals such as the Ford Capri, relying on its more precise, tidier

handling, and its quick, un-soggy steering to maintain its appeal to the traditional sports car driver suspicious of front wheel drive.

The mid-engined Monte Carlo was regarded at first as a larger, faster Fiat X1/9, but it did not enjoy the smaller car's splendid handling, having rather too much of its weight concentrated on the rear wheels. Production ceased while the designers had second thoughts, and later models were much improved. The Gamma Coupe on the other hand, with its lusty, large four cylinder engine was one of the longest-legged and refined Grand Touring cars in the medium-price range. Pininfarina beat off the Bertone challenge with the Gamma, a beautiful two door style which proved such a success that a four door 'stretched' version was produced as an alternative to the rather plain saloon.

Following the Fiat takeover, the Beta Coupe maintained Lancia's tradition of radicalism by having all-round independent suspension using MacPherson struts, and a transversely-mounted twin-cam engine driving the front wheels. The engine was offset to the right of the car, and the five speed gearbox to the left.

Lotus

In any age, in any sphere of endeavour, Anthony Colin Bruce Chapman would have achieved great things. He reversed the old aphorism about the thing being to take part, not to win. Chapman would never have understood the idea of taking part in anything without winning. He could be at best competitive and at worst downright aggressive. No designer ever had such a talent for getting to grips with things. No designer ever led where so many others were forced to follow.

Motor racing and the creation of sports cars won Chapman fame and fortune in the latter part of the twentieth century. They made him a millionaire by the time he was forty, and his racing cars gained nearly sixty Grand Prix victories before he reached fifty. His enterprises were in turn blighted and blessed, but showed a great capacity for survival. His reputation as an innovative engineer, with a flair for style and a trace of daring, is secure.

The high-flying story of Lotus is firmly that of Chapman. He was at the controls when Lotus Engineering took off in 1952 from a lock-up garage in Muswell Hill, North London, and at once almost crashed. But his genius for solving problems by going back to first principles was vital. Every Lotus began with a clean sheet of paper. Nothing was pre-conceived, no pattern followed, every feature was examined: absolutely nothing was ever incorporated in a Lotus out of habit. In due course, the rest of the world usually followed, disconcerted at not having thought of things first.

Chapman's daring was demonstrated in the Lotus Elite of 1957. For a small, struggling firm making racing cars to produce a series-production car at all was adventurous, but to make it almost entirely from glass reinforced plastic looked almost reckless. The Elite's self-supporting plastics monocoque made it a noisy car, but its handling was exemplary and it quickly became a classic. Its fine proportions and neat interior trim demonstrated that Chapman's aptitude for style extended further than the finish of the mechanical parts. He even gave his racing cars a well-planned, highly-developed appearance — and thus a useful psychological advantage over the opposition.

The Elite's exasperating unreliability reflected shortcomings of detail, however. Most of them were in any case built from kits by amateurs. Chapman hit on this as a way of outflanking British Purchase Tax regulations. He was adept at reading rule books to the letter, rather than merely the spirit, but it gave many an Elite an indifferent start in life.

Chapman was artful rather than cunning, although Lotus owners who found service problematical and spares expensive drew their own conclusions. There was never an elaborate network of efficient dealers such as Porsche would build up, and having read the eulogies of the press, most owners probably expected too much of what were basically rather fragile, highly-bred and sometimes temperamental racing cars.

The first production Lotus, the first stressed-plastic car, the first with Chapman struts at the rear to reach the private buyer — the Elite's road holding brought the great strides that had been made on the track home to the sports car customer of the Fifties.

Revelation in reinforced glass fibre. Just as the Elan +2S 130/5 seemed to reach maturity as a reliable, fast, economical Grand Tourer, it was discontinued. One of the few Lotus road cars to acquire a good name for good service, late examples of the model remained in demand long after production ceased in 1974. The polished wood fascia harks back to the days of the bespoke coachbuilder, whose customers expected such refinement. Lotus were unusual in providing it, together with the full array of instruments which sports car buyers certainly preferred. Transmission hump between the seats conceals backbone chassis frame. Taking a leaf out of Ferrari's book, the red crackle finish of the cam covers marks the Lotus Big Valve engine, which gave post-1971 cars the 115bhp of the Elan Sprint, and a top speed of over 125mph.

above

The Elan chassis was conceived as a simple test-frame for the suspension. It worked so well that plans for an all-plastic Elan were scrapped, and the backbone chassis was developed and put into production instead. At the front, the Lotus twin-cam engine with two twin-choke Weber carburettors, and rack and pinion steering; at the rear, independent suspension by Chapman struts.

above right

Fastback, down-market version of the exclusive Elite 2, the Lotus Eclat had a grp body moulded in halves by a process which enabled Lotus to form some of the largest one-piece plastic mouldings ever made on a successful production basis.

Lotus may not have been in a condition of perpetual crisis exactly, but it was regarded with some suspicion by prescriptive financiers. Nevertheless the Seven, which pre-dated even the Elite, proved to be one of the world's longest-selling sports cars, beginning its career in 1957 as a bargain-basement exemplar of good road holding, and carrying on into the Eighties, made in limited numbers by Caterham Cars, once a Lotus dealer. Caterham were given the rights by Chapman when Lotus moved up-market with the Elan series, which replaced the Elite in 1962-63.

Chapman had intended that his new car should continue the all-plastic theme of its predecessor, despite the difficulties of curing the new material. But during development, a jury-rig backbone frame was cobbled-up to test out the suspension components. It worked so well that it became the basis not only for all subsequent Lotus road sports cars, but also for the later, and much larger Delorean.

The Elan had a Ford-based four cylinder engine with the Lotus twin cam head designed for the first Lotus Cortina. It was mounted in the frame at the front, where the backbone divided. Ford also supplied the gearbox and final drive, but the rear suspension was independent by coil springs, lower wishbones and the combined spring and damper arrangement known as Chapman struts.

The Elan was not only light on its feet, it was light on petrol as well. Con-

sumptions of 30 mpg were by no means uncommon, but once again detail finish was often poor, and reliability problems cropped up. The fold-away headlamps were a constant source of trouble as were the rubber drive-shaft couplings, although these were improved in subsequent models — S2 in 1964, S3 in 1965-66, S4 in the spring of 1968, and the Sprint models from 1971 until the Elan was phased out in 1973.

The Elan Plus 2 lasted from 1967 until 1974, a 2+2 development of the Elan, and arguably the best Lotus ever. In its final form, with the 126 bhp Big Valve engine, five speed gearbox, and luxurious trim, it was known as the Plus 2S 130/5 and was an almost matchless Grand Tourer at a time when motorways were opening up the Continent and were still mostly un-speed-limited, though the cost of fuel was starting its upward spiral. The Plus 2S would cruise in fifth gear at up to 120 mph, give 28 mpg, and its reliability problems had been almost solved when the time came for it too to be superseded.

The mid-engined Europa ran in parallel with the Elans between 1967 and 1975, when it gave way to the move towards more expensive cars, later to be regretted and even reversed in an effort to improve production volumes. The first Europa had a Renault 16 engine behind the driver, cradled in a rearward fork of the backbone frame. But the front-wheel-drive Renault had the engine behind the driven wheels, while in the Europa it was ahead, so it was

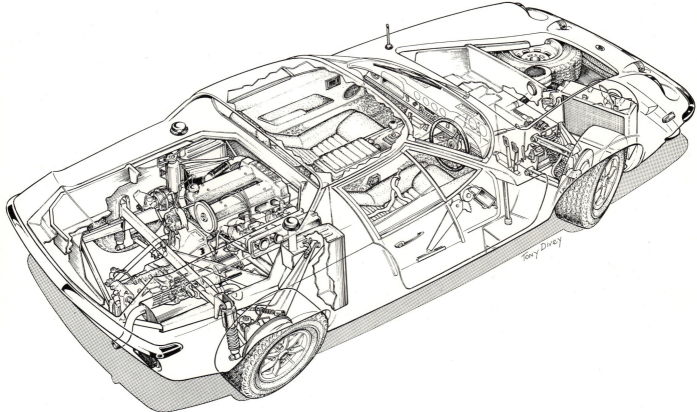

necessary to reverse the final drive gearing in order to produce four forward speeds and one reverse, and not the other way round.

Conceived as a latter-day Lotus Seven, the Europa was cheap, but inevitably, with such superlative cornering power, it grew up; on later models the grp body, formerly bonded to the frame, became detachable from it, and when Lotus began building their own engines it gained a Twin Cam, giving some models over 120 mph.

The Elan's successors were the new Elite and Eclat, highly sophisticated, stylish, and expensive. The techniques

Layout for a mid-engined coupe. The Lotus Europa featured a backbone frame with the engine behind the driver. At the front, the spare wheel was pushed to one side to accommodate the radiator.

It takes a lot to get a Lotus Esprit as out of shape as this — even if it has the power of the turbocharged engine to help the rear wheels lose their grip. Approaching the ultimate in cornering ability, the mid-engined Esprit in Essex livery acquires the colours, as well as the character, of a Team Lotus racing car.

of making the grp body structure had improved immensely over the years, but the backbone chassis remained. Lotus's own slant-four engine might have become one half of a V-8 in the fullness of time had the oil crises not intervened. As it was, Lotus moved into the upper price bracket just as the upper price bracket almost ceased to exist . . .

Yet the customary Lotus virtues of ride and handling, together with a

brilliant performance and striking lines, remained unblemished: the rakish looks and pop-up headlamps continued to be the hallmarks of the car that reflected the genius of the most innovative racing car designer ever.

Lotus even attained the star status of having the matchless Giugiaro design a show car based on the Europa. This was the Esprit, and in time it reached production as a dramatic, wedge-shaped

supercar-in-miniature, with the 16-valve 2 litre engine, and a top speed of more than 130 mph.

The market was less than kind to Lotus. Its contraction in the Seventies probably prevented the make reaching the maturity shown by Ferrari, for example, who benefitted from an earlier start. Neither did it gain the quality image of Porsche, the result perhaps of Chapman's indifference to his early customers and his obsession with designing out weight rather than building in reliability.

The later, more expensive cars largely put matters right, but by then, perhaps, a little of the grace was gone, the sense of style (except for the Esprit) had become stolid — and the heavy hand of the legislative draughtsmen had frozen the blossoming Lotus before it had had a chance to reach full flower.

Maserati

In their first twenty-five years of producing sports cars, Maserati could hardly have been accused of flooding the market. Nearly all their products were really for racing, and only a few hundred were made. From 1926 till the early Fifties they never designed any car intended to be used on the road.

Yet in that delightful cross-breeding which maintained the racing car's relationship with the sports car, many Maseratis were equipped with lights, mudguards, a few appurtenances to satisfy the law, and were used with vigour and enthusiasm on the highways of Europe and North America. Unfortunately, by 1938 the founding brothers Carlo, Bindo, Alfieri, Ettore, and Ernesto were either dead or getting on in life. The surviving brothers sold out the Officine Alfieri Maserati to the big Orsi industrial group, which kept them on,

producing racing cars until the debut of the A6G sports car, a 6 cylinder single overhead cam of 1½ litres and 2 litres. This was shown at one of the first post-war motor shows, Geneva in 1947, before the Maseratis left to form OSCA in Bologna in an effort to regain their independence.

Following the example of Ferrari, and in tune with the economic conditions of the time, Count Omer Orsi got the factory to take the racing engine and adapt it for road use as well. By 1950 the A6 had appeared as a two door coupe with Pininfarina bodywork along the lines of his famous Cisitalia, incorporating the Maserati radiator grille already well known on the superb-looking but not very reliable 4CLT 'San Remo' Grand Prix cars. Other versions of the A6-engined road car followed, with bodies by Allemano, Frua, and Zagato, but the numbers remained small.

It was not until 1957, with the introduction of the 3500 model, that Maserati

By 1957 Maserati were having to pick British brains to compete at Le Mans. This bulbous 450S coupe, shared by Stirling Moss and Harry Schell, had a body designed by Lotus aerodynamicist Frank Costin. Its V-8 engine would not rev, the inside overheated the drivers, an oil pipe broke, and the drivers were relieved when the transmission failed after four hours.

appeared to take the market for road-going sports or GT cars seriously. The racing programme had been highly successful both in sports cars, with the A6GCS and the 300S, and in Formula 1, where the 250F had already won Fangio half his 1954 world championship and was about to win him another.

But the cost had been enormous. Like many before and since, Maserati found the financial burden crippling, aggravated by the loss of an entire team of cars in accidents during the Venezuelan Grand Prix of 1957. Furthermore, Orsi lost money following default of payments for goods supplied to Argentina, so racing had to stop. The market place had to come first.

Racing's loss was the car connoisseur's gain, however. Whilst the production of racing cars for sale did not cease, as witness the amazing 'birdcage' Maseratis designed by Alfieri largely from scrap 250F and old sports car components, new road cars were a

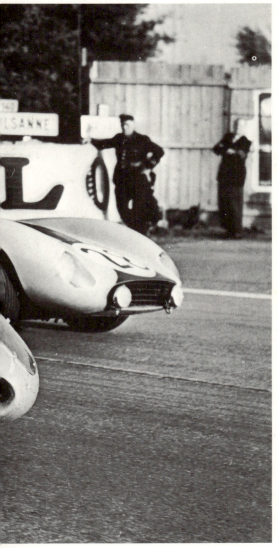

priority, and the following years saw them in bewildering variety.

Basically the engines comprised the old A6 six cylinder, ranging from 2 litres to just over 4 litres, and a V-8 from 4.2 to 4.9 litres. For the most part, chassis construction followed the norm for the Modenese small-series production sports and GT car, namely a frame of large diameter tubes, independent front suspension, and a live axle or occasionally de Dion at the rear. Maserati only made the chassis at first; bodywork was left to one of the classic Italian coachbuilding houses such as Vignale. The cars were fast, powerful and exciting, but they neither handled as well as the equivalent Ferrari, nor were ever very quiet or refined, unlike the new Lamborghini coming along to challenge them. They were expensive and hand-built, however, bore one of motor racing's proudest names, and were exclusive enough to appeal to a rich set of people who valued individuality and new means of expressing their wealth above almost anything.

The 3500 GT, GTI, and Sebring appeared in long-chassis, relatively luxurious form, or short-chassis, with lightweight, rather racier bodies. Touring made most of the 2,000 or so built between 1958 and 1964, except for the pretty Vignale Sebring, named after the occasion when the 450S won the important 12 Hours race there in 1957. Capable of nearly 140 mph with 235 bhp, the Sebring gave way in 1963 to the Mistrale.

This turned out to be the last of the rather noisy six cylinder cars, although it was a successful model, with a six year production run of nearly 1,000.

The first of the V-8s was the rather more exclusive 5000 GT. The first three of these used up engines left over from the racing programme, but the remaining 29 had a de-tuned version under development for the more numerous Quattroporte (four door), Mexico, and Ghibli models. The tubular frame was stiffened by steel sheet panelling, production numbers increased, yet still the economics of making high-class cars for a fickle, fashion-conscious market failed to add up, and in 1968 Citroen took a controlling interest, in the expectation of putting the name and the engineering reputation to better use.

Meanwhile, the thunderous V-8 was installed in the front-engined Indy, which departed from the traditional chassis entirely, being a unit-construction car of immense speed. It was

x

x

x

x

x

x

x

x

x

x

x

x

x

x

One of the handful of late Italian supercars to have the engine at the front, the Maserati Khamsin is available with either the popular ZF five speed manual gearbox, or a fully automatic Borg Warner.

followed in 1973 by the Khamsin, which also broke with tradition by being bodied by Bertone. The V-8 also went into the mid-engined Bora, with a body not only styled but also engineered in the Ital Design studios of the ubiquitous Giugiaro.

Citroen technology contributed to the Bora's rather less powerful sister car, the Merak. What the French company had really wanted from the relationship with Maserati was a short-cut to a V-6 engine for a sporty prestige car they were planning, called initially Citroen-Maserati. The engine they had in mind was three-quarters of the Maserati V-8, although it came out rather differently. In due course they were able to con-

tribute to other aspects of Maseratis, the Merak for example using the front-drive transmission developed for the SM, altered to drive the rear wheels, and the high-pressure Citroen hydraulics for its brakes.

The partnership came to an end in 1973, and following the fuel crisis, Maserati almost stopped dead in its tracks. It took Government help to put Alessandro de Tomaso in charge, and production resumed in 1976, yet a certain amount of the Citroen legacy remained. The liaison did illustrate something a number of small, specialist sports car makers were able to exploit, however. Even large combines some-times have a requirement for quick,

Mercedes-Benz

Perhaps only Rolls-Royce have ever been able to match the reputation of Mercedes-Benz for engineering excellence. Complexity has never been regarded as a reason for not pursuing a design principle if it was felt worthwhile. So, when engineers at the world's oldest-established car maker decided to develop the notion of the space frame, nothing was allowed to stand in their way.

The multi-tube frame, with all the tubes straight, and none subject to bending or torsional stresses, was a radical departure in the Forties when it was conceived as the sports car structure of the future.

Germany had still not been wholly accepted back into the international community following the war, but Mercedes-Benz did want to demonstrate that they had not lost their touch in motor racing. A return to the track in a modest way would help sales and prestige, but as they were to see in 1951, the year Germany was re-admitted to the Federation Internationale de l'Automobile, it was of little use to rely on out-dated designs in a new world. A 2 litre Ferrari soundly beat the old W 163 Mercedes-Benz in the Argentine Temporada.

It seemed to Prince von Urach in charge of research, designer Rudolph Uhlenhaut, and Technical Director Fritz Nallinger that a new approach was necessary. This was the carefully triangulated structure, equipped with the 3 litre engine from the 300S luxury saloon, known as the 300 SL, or *Sport Leicht*. It abounded with novelty. The demands of the framework meant that the occupants had to climb in over high sills so, with a coupe top, conventional doors became impossible. Uhlenhaut equipped it instead with the famous gullwing doors. The engine was inclined at 50° to bring the overall height down and keep the centre of gravity low. The aerodynamics were smooth and slippery and the top speed of around 150 mph, despite a relatively heavy cast-iron cylinder block, was formidable, even with the early 171 bhp carburettor engine.

The 300 SL was a propaganda victory before it ever turned a wheel. The Germans' pre-war reputation for overwhelming efficiency on the race track was undiminished. After they finished second and fourth in their first race, the

intuitive engineering. Lotus, Maserati, and Ferrari were all able to act in a consultative or creative capacity for large-scale manufacturers, while Porsche in particular made a resounding commercial success of designing components, or sometimes complete cars, for the world's motor industry—often unacknowledged and carried out covertly.

The years may have derided the old notion that the racing car of today is tomorrow's sports car, and the touring car of the day after, but specialist manufacturers often proved to have something to offer the volume side of the industry, as a result of searching for the very best in speed or performance for the bespoke part of the market.

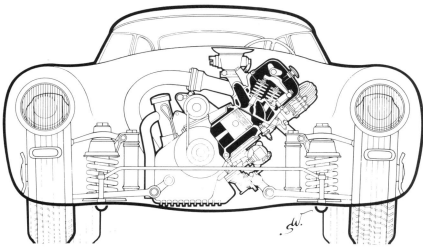

top
The gull-wing doors of the production 300 SL Mercedes-Benz (shown here) extended to a lower sill level than the racing prototypes, into which the driver could only climb with some difficulty. The large spare did not leave much space in the 'boot' for luggage.

above
The Mercedes-Benz 300 engine, complete with pushrods and carburettors, was laid over on its side to reduce the bonnet height and centre of gravity on the 300SL sports car.

1952 Mille Miglia, their principal rival in the next race at Berne, a 4.1 litre Ferrari, broke its transmission on the start line. The Mercs took the first three places. The usually imperturbable Jaguar team rushed into hasty modifications of the XK 120C's cooling system for Le Mans. The Jaguars went out with overheating; Mercedes came first and second. Even they were surprised. At the Nurburgring 1000 Kilometres, they scored a line-ahead 1-2-3-4, then took first and second in the Carrera Panamericana.

In fact the car was far from perfect. Despite the ingenious space frame it was by no means light, and the factory's rather stubborn devotion to swing-axle rear suspension, even of the low-pivot type, made the car very tricky to handle. A change of mind half way through a corner demanded driving skill of the highest order to avert disaster as the wheel camber changed, the tyres went 'on edge', and the grip suddenly diminished. Yet the design was so successful that it set the pattern of development for the W 196 Grand Prix car, and its sports-racing derivative the 300 SLR.

Here was a monument to an engineering philosophy which decreed that nothing should be left to chance: not so much as the closing of a valve left to the vagaries of a spring. Valve closure on the 300 SLR was by a desmodromic arrangement whose complexity and precision were matched only by its efficiency and expense. Eight cylinders, the crankshaft running in ten bearings — a Hirth built-up crankshaft and roller bearings naturally — fuel injection, turbo-cooled inboard brakes front and rear, a ZF gearbox in unit with the final drive; nothing, it seemed, had been overlooked. True, the swing-axles remained, and the factory did not yet consider disc brakes sufficiently developed, invoking instead the somewhat clumsy air-brake which created such controversy at Le Mans. Fuel was alcohol, laced with less potent brews according to the requirements of individual races.

The career of the 300 SLR was cut short by the Le Mans disaster, yet it scored overwhelming victories at its

other appearances in 1955. It gained a 1-2 in the Mille Miglia, perhaps the greatest drive of Stirling Moss's career. It came first, second and third in the TT at Dundrod; first, second and fourth in the Targa Florio; first in the Swedish Grand Prix and in the Eifel Grand Prix on the Nurburgring.

Sadly, the 300 SLRs were then to become museum pieces. The cruel accident at Le Mans, the blazing magnesium as Pierre Levegh's car crashed into the crowd, sealed its fate at the very beginning of its development. The 300 SL appeared in production form, as gull-wing coupes up to 1956, thereafter open roadsters with normal doors until withdrawn in 1962.

The space frame had been expensive to make, and too fragile in even a minor accident ever to be appropriate for a sports car in the rough and tumble of the real world, and Mercedes-Benz never repeated the experiment.

Mercedes' other sporting cars of the Fifties were somewhat less splendid, the 190 SL being a worthy tourer based on the 180 and 220 series of saloon cars between 1954 and 1962 — much the same period as the 300 SL. The pair were

replaced by the 230 SL based on a series of saloons with a six cylinder single overhead camshaft engine which began as a 2.3 litre and was progressively enlarged to 2.5, then 2.8 litres until it too was replaced in 1971. Conservatively styled, with a distinctive dip in the line of its coupe roof, this was a fast, extremely civilized car with a good turn of speed — around 125 mph — and a low pivot point which seemed to tame the swing-axle arrangement somewhat.

It was succeeded by the even more refined 350 SL and 450 SLC, once again based on the S-Series saloons with a wide choice over the years of twin-cam six cylinder and V-8 engines with fuel injection giving up to 240 bhp.

As sports cars, these top Mercedes were masterpieces of understatement. They were neither cheap nor economical, and their comfort and handling attained the superlative standards of a dynasty which not only traced its ancestors to the very dawn of the motor car, but also had a competitive career spanning its entire history. So long as there were sports cars, there was a Mercedes-Benz to epitomize the very best in the state of the art.

Following the Wagnerian 300SL and 300SLR, the 190SL and the 230SL (shown here) appeared almost timid. Yet they were amongst the best road cars of their time, sure-footed, smooth, and quiet.

The MG TC was little more than the pre-war TA or TB, with little attempt at bringing it up to date. Despite cart springs and a pushrod engine, it became the pattern for the postwar sports car, particularly in America.

MG

More people have probably discovered good handling, precise steering, and the sheer fun of driving at the wheel of an MG than any place else. Few cars have come to be regarded with such affection, and perhaps no car has gained such a following of enthusiasts who will set up clubs, hold meetings and compare notes any time, anywhere in the world. No car has had so many imperfections acknowledged with such glee as 'character', and no sports car was turned out in such numbers, for so long.

The roots of MG lay in the Twenties, when Cecil Kimber was the manager of Morris Garages and identified a market for what we might nowadays ungraciously call tarted-up Morrises. The establishment of the make was assured at least partly through the worthiness of

the components, which were inherited from the Morris range. They were assembled with one eye to style and another to performance, reinforced by a competition programme which persuaded the customers that the cheap little two seater they were buying really had an identity of its own. It managed to rise above its relatively humble origins through racing and record-breaking, to acquire an elusive status which suited the class-conscious English admirably. Kimber, astute observer of the market that he was, made it a cheap car that even rich people bought because they liked it, anticipating a phenomenon that made the Mini a car for the ragged and the Royal thirty years later.

In common with most European manufacturers, MG found themselves with little choice after the war but to start up again where they had left off - making the T-series Midget open two

had the sporting cachet that came from racing, or the reflected glory of Col. Goldie Gardner's 200 mph on the Dessau autobahn.

There were of course other MG models to choose from in the Thirties, but by the time the TC, virtually identical to the TB, came out in October 1945, it stood alone. It was difficult enough obtaining the raw materials for one car, let alone a whole range. Indeed almost the only way to ensure an allocation of supplies was to export, and MG took the opportunity to sell cars seriously in America for the first time.

The response was immediate and far-reaching. America discovered the sports car through the MG, and where MG ventured, the rest of Europe's motor industry was not far behind. Despite the regard in which America held the TC, rivals soon showed up its shortcomings — and they were manifest. It was not enough for Clark Gable, Briggs Cunningham, John Fitch, and Phil Hill to have MGs, they needed to be just a little faster to avoid the indignity of being out-accelerated by the new, powerful generation emerging from Detroit. It was certainly necessary to

Inheriting a famous name and reputation, the 1969 MG Midget grew close to its soon-to-be-discontinued look-alike, the Austin-Healey Sprite. The bureaucratic hand of BL decreed adoption of a corporate style which meant a rather featureless oval grille. Worse was to come in 1974, when the 'soft-nosed' bumpers appeared, spoiling both the appearance and the handling of one of the world's best-loved small sports cars.

seater. This had been regarded as something of a retrograde step in 1936, when the TA appeared with a pushrod engine instead of the unhappily discontinued Morris overhead cam unit. Furthermore it was a 1,292cc long-stroke unit, the car was bigger than the Midget it replaced, and as further evidence of its decadence, it even had a synchromesh gearbox.

Each succeeding generation of MG enthusiasts was to be similarly offended by repeated corruptions of their cherished institution.

A parallel pressed steel frame, with half-elliptic springs front and rear, a slow-revving four cylinder engine (even when succeeded by the shorter-stroke TB in 1939) and a top speed of a mere 80 mph may appear an unpromising specification for a sports car, but not many small saloons of the day could keep up, few were as 'nippy', and none

The TD was an enhancement in handling and a rather more worthy car than the TC even though it discarded the traditional wire wheels, and it offered rather more comfort. By 1953, however, the TF would be derided by Tom McCahill in *Mechanix Illustrated* as 'Mrs Cadey's dead cat slightly warmed over.' Yet all became classics, highly prized by enthusiasts — and expensive.

improve the handling so that they might at least catch up on the corners.

Change was inevitable, and by the end of 1949 the TC had given way to the TD. Once again, MG dyed-in-the-wool enthusiasts found it an affront. This time, they avowed, the car really had gone soft. It had independent front suspension, a supple ride (it was not: they only thought it was) and pressed steel disc wheels. It even had bumpers.

To the traditionalists' astonishment, it sold better than ever. The wider-spaced gear ratios, the extra weight, the increased width, and the larger-section tyres made no difference. In fact the new car was superior in most respects, particularly the steering, now rack and pinion, and it was faster as well. By 1953 it had evolved into the TF, barely more than a facelift at a time when the Triumph TR2 and the Austin-Healey

100 were offering greatly superior performance for much the same money. Moreover the TR and the Healey looked like cars of the Sixties, whereas the MG remained essentially one of the Thirties despite the coachbuilt, wood-framed quality of the body, and the strength of its good name.

The entire history of the Abingdon-on-Thames factory was bedevilled by managerial indifference till the end. Successive managements, from Kimber's on, had to deal first with Lord Nuffield, who regarded the sports car with distaste, then with BMC and Leonard Lord, who kept championing rivals such as Austin-Healey, and finally with BL, whose cost accountants killed it off. Investment in new models was never forthcoming because the market was relatively small. Yet who knows what volumes MG could have achieved had cash been put behind some of the enterprising schemes for mid-engined and other sports cars drawn up by MG?

After much badgering, BMC finally gave way and let Abingdon produce the MGA in 1955. It had a power deficit against the Healeys and the TRs, to which the unfortunate 115 mph Twin-Cam version proved unequal. Unreliability forced MG back to the pushrod engine, with which the MGA could barely reach 100 mph. The handling was superior to either of its rivals, and with a strong, scuttle-braced chassis frame it was probably safer and stiffer as well. A racing version did well at Le Mans, but after the 1955 disaster a nervous management failed to exploit the opportunities racing offered, and the programme was stopped.

A new Midget based on the Austin-Healey Sprite was introduced in 1961, followed by the MGB, which was to run for the next 17 years through various marks and forms, including the closed GT. There was the abortive six cylinder MGC intended to replace the big Austin-Healey 3000, but which suffered from under-development before being axed due to disappointing sales. Management indifference also proved the death-knell of the fastest MG ever, the Rover-engined V-8, a stirring 125 mph coupe which was to become one of the most sought-after of all classic MGs.

Laden with squashy bumpers, their ride-height adjusted to meet US regulations and ruining the handling, their relatively small engines emasculated by emission control equipment essential to the American market, MG went into decline by the middle Seventies. Their position in the market place was snatched gratefully by Datsun amongst others, and many promising designs by gifted but frustrated engineeers were abandoned. The plight of BL meant closure of the factory, and by 1980 the last 'real' MGs were passing into the folklore of the motor car.

left
Late in arriving, but nonetheless welcome, the open MGA was supplemented by this fixed-head version. The door handles were neat pull-up catches which could be operated with one finger.

below
Fastest-ever MG was the Rover V-8 engined version of the familiar MGB GT. In 1973 guise, before the introduction of the soft-nosed models a year later, it had the style and pace of many more expensive cars.

Strictly in tune with tradition, the Morgan 4/4 had a four cylinder engine, giving a lively rather than dramatic performance, quite in keeping with the flavour of a living period piece. The leather bonnet strap was optional to add a touch of Le Mans, where the regulations demanded it.

Morgan

The pace of change at Morgan was never very fast. It took over 25 years for Morgans to acquire a fourth wheel. It was another 20 before Lucas's refusal to make any more free-standing head-lamps brought about the first styling change. Morgan did not set about making replica Vintage sports cars — they never stopped making the real thing. They used much the same techniques and materials, even employed some of the same personnel or their descendants, to make much the same car as they had been making in the Thirties, when the 4/4 augmented the range of three wheelers they had been making since 1910.

The Founder H. F. S. Morgan, was born at Stoke Lacey Rectory, Hereford, in 1881. His father was the Rev. Prebendary H. G. Morgan, and he married the daughter of the Rev. Archibald Day, formerly the vicar of St Matthias, Malvern Link. With so many ecclesiastics involved, Morgan's moral heritage was secure. Its financial status was good too, with the Rev. Prebendary Morgan putting

up £3,000 to get production started, and funding the little red-brick factory in Pickersleigh Road which opened in 1919. Yet Morgan was only one of a multitude of cottage industry car makers who took advantage of the booming years when the world was getting on to its wheels.

The three wheelers from the picturesque Malvern Hills were determinedly working-class. They were modest, economical, reliable, and slow. Less proletarian than the traditional motor cycle and sidecar, they were amongst the very first production cars in the world (together with Sizaire-Naudin) to have independent front suspension. Since the weight was under 7 cwt they were taxed as tricycles — the same as a motor cycle combination — but this was a peculiarly British concession, and there was no market to speak of anywhere else.

Yet the Morgan did become known abroad. The temptation to put a big engine into this light, strong frame proved too great, and Morgans were soon into racing and record-breaking. The car which won the 1913 Cyclecar Grand Prix at Amiens weighed a mere 3 cwt, and laid down the principles of the fearsome Grand Prix Morgans, with their enormous Vee-twin motorcycle engines, capable of 115 mph.

By 1936 the three-wheeler market was declining; the mass-production lines of Ford, Austin and Morris were competing with the artisans and craftsmen in the depths of Worcestershire. It was straightforward enough to give the F-Type three-wheeler a rear axle, abandon chain drive, and exhibit the 4/4 (four wheels, four cylinders) at the London and Paris Motor Shows. A sporting connection was not forgotten, however, and a 1,098cc overhead inlet valve Coventry-Climax engined Morgan competed at Le Mans in 1938, qualifying for the Biennial Cup.

The sliding pillar independent front suspension system was retained. Lancia had adopted it as just about the only practical means, given the metallurgy and knowledge of the time, for keeping the wheels upright and independent, and it served Morgan well, suitably strengthened and subtly developed but in principle still the same, throughout their history. The chassis was composed of Z-section steel members, and the gearbox was separate from the engine, in the middle of the car.

Morgan remained small, surviving the Thirties when so many of its competitors went to the wall, and relying heavily, as ever, on buying in major items such as engines, gearboxes, and axles from specialists. Salisbury gears,

Standard Motor Company, Coventry-Climax, and Moss carried out the machining and capital-intensive operations; Morgan at Malvern Link ash-framed the body, hand-rolled and panel-beat, in a works which changed hardly at all from the Twenties. It harked back to a forgotten tradition, when workmanship and pride had more of a place in the scheme of things. When customers called they discovered a fragment of industrial archaeology that had somehow survived, like the caelocanth, into an age to which its contemporaries had never aspired.

Yet the Morgan was not completely anachronistic. It had to bend a little to change, for example every time its engine supply was threatened. The 2,088cc Standard Vanguard engine was introduced in 1950, and the resultant increase in power not only transformed the performance, but changed the name to Plus 4. This gave way in turn to the TR2 engine, which made it even faster, in 1954. Better handling than the TR made the Plus 4 Morgan a formidable competitor in rallies, and Triumph became aware of the competition both here and in the market place. The engine supply was reduced for a time, and Morgan brought back the 4/4 with a rather feeble Ford engine.

Yet it was the Plus 4 which made the Morgan reputation for Vintage-style handling, along with a performance which was at least a match for the

Only fifty Morgan Coupes were ever made. The Plus-four-Plus not only had a coupe roof, but unlike any other Morgan it had a lockable boot. Enthusiasts seemed to prefer the more traditionally styled car.

The big Rover V-8 was a snug fit in the narrow Morgan bonnet. Plus Eights await finishing in the tiny factory at Malvern Link, in the heart of rural Worcestershire.

moderns. It combined the best of both worlds; it was Vintage without tears.

But the days of the four cylinder Triumph were numbered, and by 1968 it was necessary to develop a new flagship. This was the Morgan Plus 8, with a Rover V-8 engine, still in the familiar Z-section chassis, with the underslung rear axle, and the archaic-looking but effective sliding pillar ifs. The body was still ash-framed, and although it was a little wider, the shape was unchanged.

At 125 mph it was the fastest Morgan ever, and the most dramatic. It was the Grand Prix Morgan of the Seventies, with hairy-chested handling, and road performance more likely to be limited by the skill and daring of the driver than by the capabilities of the car. It was best driven open, because the cutaway doors allowed the elbows to overflow the body sides, which was a help with the heavy steering. Like all Morgans it gave the driver a seat-of-the-pants feeling such as pilots get in Tiger Moths or sailors in a well-trimmed racing dinghy.

The firm springing makes the long bonnet of a Morgan bob up and down over bumps, and the occupants follow suit. The hoods were never very satisfactory, and in the wet drops of water tended to run down the inside of the windscreen, but like the keen, wide-eyed enthusiasts who imported the first MGs to America, Morgan drivers tended to think all sports cars were like this, and was it not part of the charm . . . ?

Like malt whisky, Morgans are an acquired taste: pungent, distinctive, yet subtle, and varying — a taste you never stop learning about, never fail to appreciate. You can wear a Morgan like a crumpled suit, reassuring, familiar, comfortable. Or you can wear it in the King's Road, ever-trendy, never unfashionable, the hallmark of good taste with a dash of hair-shirt virility — all the features that sports car lovers love, and sports car haters love to hate.

Peter Morgan, who took over when HFS died in 1959, never changed the Morgan philosophy, even in the late Fifties and early Sixties when it was beginning to look old fashioned. Nostalgia took over where habit left off, and far from going into decline, the Morgan order book remained full when others, despite frantically trying to keep abreast of the times, were emptying.

While it was true that almost every component was changed, strengthened, improved, and altered over the years and for different models (the Ford-engined 4/4 was later given more power), the car itself preserved a unique continuity, making it one of the longest-lived classics in the history of the car.

Pegaso

There was no doubt what Ferrari thought when he heard that a Spanish lorry manufacturer was building cars fit to rival his. Ferrari had a long memory, and still smarted over his dismissal from Alfa Romeo before the war. He blamed this on a certain engineer, and in a famous outburst criticized this engineer's designs for an engine whose crankshaft 'revolved like a skipping rope,' and a racing car which was 'outdated, good only for scrap or a museum' (and moreover, killed its test driver). 'With sleek, oiled hair and smart clothes that he wore with a somewhat levantine elegance,' Ferrari wrote afterwards, 'he affected jackets with sleeves that came far down below his wrists, and shoes with enormously thick rubber soles.' The reason for the thick soles, this engineer explained to Ferrari, was because, 'A great engineer's brain should not be jolted by the inequalities of the ground and consequently needed to be carefully sprung.'

It said a good deal more for Wilfredo Ricart's sense of humour than Enzo Ferrari's that he was taken seriously. Even Vittorio Jano described Ricart as a man of profound intellect. It is true that some of his designs were monuments of complexity, sometimes even impractical, but the same was probably said of Leonardo da Vinci. His fatal Alfa Romeo 512 was a horizontally opposed 12 cylinder, rear-engined racing car with a centrifugal supercharger giving 335 bhp from 1½ litres. He had already abandoned the Type 162, which was a 3 litre planned to give 560 bhp, with two carburettors, 3 stage supercharging with five compressors, 16 cylinders, and 64 valves. By 1940 he was working on a 4-bank 28 cylinder radial aero-engine, and the following year designed a unitary construction road car for postwar production with all independent suspension, a twin-cam 2 litre engine, and a gearbox integral with the final drive — a radical layout not unlike that eventually adopted for the Alfetta Coupe of 1974.

In 1945 Ricart left Alfa Romeo and returned to his native Spain, joining the Government-backed Empresa Nacional de Autocamiones SA, in Barcelona. ENASA were to build Pegaso trucks and buses in the old Hispano-Suiza works, but Ricart's job was to include the design of a new car, a technical exercise to demonstrate that Spain could make cars which were a match for anybody's.

Pegasos were impeccably thought out, and although relatively plain beside some of Ricart's other flights of fancy, they were sumptuously engineered. It was 1951 before the first appeared on show, and production only lasted until 1958 — a matter of 125 cars; the Pegaso was to remain one of the most exclusive Grande Marques ever.

The 1951 Pegaso Z 102 at the Paris motor show. The rear is raised to show off the torsion-bar-sprung de Dion rear suspension, with the integral five speed gearbox, inboard brakes, and self-locking differential which so astonished contemporary engineers.

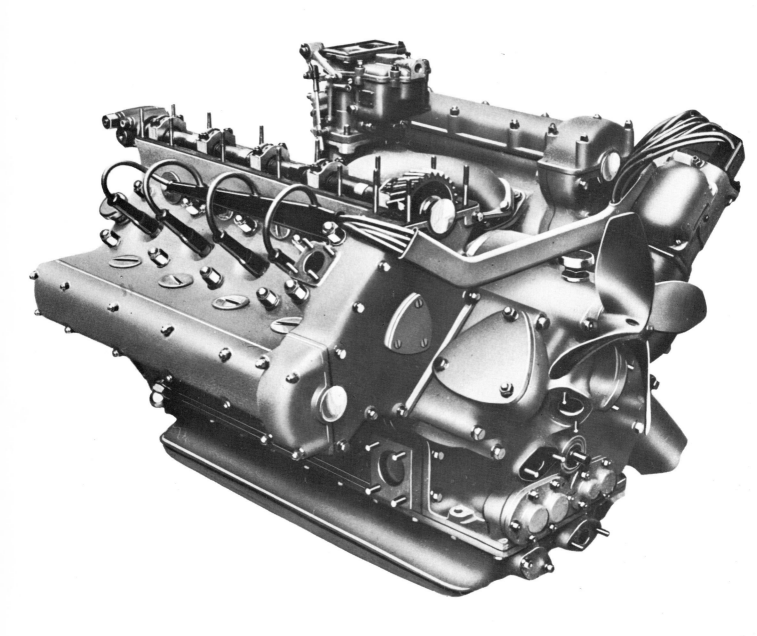

Rare picture from *Autocar's* archives of the Pegaso V-8 with the cam cover removed from one bank of cylinders, showing the gear drive.

The early editions were 2.8 litre V-8s, with four overhead camshafts, dry-sump lubrication, and as a further refinement culled from contemporary racing practice, sodium-cooled exhaust valves. The chassis design was equally advanced. It employed square section tubing, with independent suspension by torsion bars, and a de Dion rear also sprung by torsion bars.

Later Pegasos were no less sensational. The V-8 engine was enlarged, sometimes supercharged, and could be supplied in whatever state of tune the customer cared for. Bodies were designed to special order as well, mostly by the great Italian fashion houses such as Touring, or their French counterparts Saoutchik, famous for their flowing curves and rather florid chrome.

The Z 103 reverted to pushrod valve operation, but the engine was enlarged to between 4 and 4.7 litres. With Ricart's career drawing to a close, the impetus for making cars had gone, however, and ENASA stuck to the commercial vehicles which were, after all, the mainstay of their business.

Pegasos rarely appeared in sport, but they did briefly attain the distinction of being the world's fastest production cars when a Z-102 achieved 250 kph (156 mph) in 1953. Yet it was a car best remembered for its exclusiveness and the sensation it created at the motor shows of the Fifties. There, it was invariably the most flamboyant, the most stylish and sometimes the most bizarre exhibit, in an age when design for production was partly the art of the copyist. Pegaso provided an entire generation with something to copy.

Porsche

Even their most uncritical admirers often agonized over Porsche's unswerving devotion to engines which overhung the rear axle. This arrangement gave handling which to even the most charitable was different from anything else; to the uncharitable it was at best difficult, at worst dangerous. It was often described as a triumph of development over design since it managed, by virtue of suspension settings quite unlike those of other cars, to achieve immense cornering power. Yet it never quite overcame the prejudice that the balance of the car was all wrong to begin with — rather in the fashion of the earnest direction-seeker being advised not to start from here.

Yet if the basic architecture was faulty, why did succeeding generations of sports car drivers endorse the Porsche with such enthusiasm? For a substantial part of the Sixties, any meeting of the Grand Prix Drivers' Association might be taken for a branch convention of the Porsche 911 owners' club. Porsche drivers tended to be a brotherhood united by a common loyalty to the marque, and would brook no criticism beyond the indifferent interior heater or the price of spare parts.

Casting doubt on the design was like arguing the text Moses brought down from the mountain. It was inadmissible.

Colin Chapman may have set the standard for inventiveness and Enzo Ferrari for a sort of operatic bravura, but Dr Porsche provided the benchmark for execution. The cars built in the rather straggling factory at Stuttgart-Zuffenhausen were invariably models of engineering perfection. The castings were given a purposeful elegance that made the engine compartment of a Porsche a thing of beauty — particularly to beholders who had paid to enjoy the prospect.

Early Porsches were not so much designed as evolved from the materials and components available, and these were based firmly on the Volkswagen. The irrepressible genius of Dr Porsche had laid down the Auto Union racing car and the VW at a time when, with the knowledge then available, a rear engine was the logical answer to the problems of traction and weight distribution with which all known practical suspension systems were burdened.

His father not yet out of detention following collaboration with the political masters of the Third Reich, young Ferry

overleaf
overleaf
Porsche re-invented the Surrey top popularized by Triumph in the Sixties, on fears that the truly open car might be outlawed by US safety regulations. The rear window structure of the Porsche Targa carried a hoop to meet expected legislation on roll-over safety, which never materialized.

below
The prototype Porsche at Gmünd, Austria in 1948, Ferry Porsche at the wheel. Porsche had entertained the idea of a VW-based sports car before the war. Sold for 7,000 Swiss Francs in September 1948, this car was found many years later, and bought back for the Porsche museum.

Sporting Porsches. Privately entered cars were able to take part in sports car racing substantially unaltered from standard trim. On August 3, 1958, these 356 coupes took part in the 1000 Kms race round the tortuous Nurburgring.

Porsche set about creating a new sports car. The Volkswagen was the obvious basis, and any handling deficiencies the new Porsche inherited would have to be ironed out afterwards.

In due course, most of them were, but not before some models suffered from a low-speed understeer, or tendency to run wide on corners, which changed to a sudden snap of oversteer, or tail-heaviness at speed. The transition could catch out the inexperienced or the un-wary, and it was not until the 1964 911

that the problem was altogether resolved. Meanwhile, the 356 had established itself with the aerodynamic body which was to become such a classic and, as time went on, fewer and fewer Volkswagen components. The Porsche Speedster became part of the folklore on the race track. Porsche spent their promotional budget at Le Mans, the Targa Florio, Sebring and the Mille Miglia instead of buying space in the media. They knew they would reach the hearts and minds of their customers

more convincingly by the means that sports car makers know best — by competition.

Their victories were almost unparalleled, and even when they were not in the running for outright victories, such as at Le Mans, where they competed for many years in the 1½ and 2 litre category, they scored convincing class wins, and impressed with their speed and efficiency.

The 1964 car remained recognizably Porsche. It had six cylinders instead of four and the handling was improved, but it was air-cooled, and although the proportions were better, it was still unmistakable. It started as a 2 litre but got gradually bigger, producing more and more power, until the 1976 Turbo put the Porsche amongst the fastest road cars in the world. By then, the racing department had discarded the charade of making all their racing cars resemble road cars, and had built the dramatic 917 sports racing car and the 250 mph 'Porsche Panzer' Can-Am cars.

The 1969 VW-Porsche project which resulted in the unlovely and largely unloved 914 was regarded by the muscly young men who drove 'real' Porsches as an aberration. Yet its faults were not wholly of its own making; the market was probably unready for a mid-engined sports car, with its lack of luggage space and cramped interior. The idea that good handling and precise balance required some sacrifices in space and comfort had gone out, and it was not yet evident that it would have to come back in.

The car handled well and was finely engineered, but it was almost as expensive as a regular Porsche without quite being one. It was made as a joint project with VW and although that was a good idea, the 914 was not the vehicle to carry it out.

This turned out to be the 924, which not only confirmed that a joint strategy with Volkswagen could work, but put the rest of the Porsche philosophy to the test. From being air-cooled, rear-engined cars, Porsches were now water-cooled and front-engined.

From 1930, Porsche had operated principally as a design office. As such it carried out designs for cars, military equipment, engines, gearboxes, in fact almost anything of an engineering nature. The Porsche 924 started out as a project for Volkswagen-Audi to replace the ill-starred VW-Porsche 914, but emerged as a new sort of Porsche to be built not in small quantities at Zuffenhausen, but in substantial numbers at Neckarsulm. Following the tradition set by the far-sighted Cecil Kimber with MG, it used as many production parts as proved compatible with the quality and high performance Porsche owners demanded; it had a 2 litre Audi engine, VW Golf front suspension, K70 brakes, and even a rear suspension derived from the VW Beetle.

Early 924s did not receive universal acclaim on account of road noise and a rather austere interior, but with the weight at last redistributed by putting the gearbox in unit with the final drive, the handling was superb, and the 125 mph performance of the pre-turbo model highly respectable. The Turbo 924 managed well over 140 mph, with vivid acceleration and only a small fuel consumption penalty — both cars gave between 21 and 25 mpg.

But, of course the *pur-sang* Porsche enthusiasts were unhappy. To them, the 924 devalued the currency because it was no longer exclusive, and no longer

To mark the racing successes Porsche enjoyed while running under sponsorship, a special version of the 924 was sold with Martini's red, blue and black lining.

above
Fuel injection and a turbocharger put a premium on space under the bonnet of the Porsche 924. The belt-driven overhead camshaft engine lay at an angle to reduce height.

the Turbo apart) in the supercar class. In 1977, however, a year after the 924, came the 928, the most studiously designed Porsche ever produced although not without some dissenting voices inside the ranks.

Ferry Porsche fell out with Professor Ernst Fuhrmann, who headed Porsche, over the lack of room inside, also over failure of the 928 to replace the 911, which remained in demand by customers who did not want the new design. Like the 924, it had gone front-engined, with a water-cooled, fuel injected V-8 of great complexity but immense power, 240 bhp for the normal 4½ litre, 300 bhp for the 4.6 litre 928S, giving the latter a top speed in excess of 150 mph.

Porsches may have less emotional appeal than Ferraris, but they score heavily on technical merit and efficiency. They may be put together with less passion, but they are engineered with all the precision that thorough German technicians can give them. More imposing than elegant, Porsches inspire admiration rather than affection, respect rather than attachment, yet they may still go down in history as the greatest sports car of all time.

above
In an effort to achieve good weight distribution, Porsche put the gearbox in unit with the final drive of the 924 model, which has a rear window opening to provide access to the luggage platform.

right
Like the 924, the Porsche 928 has the gearbox in unit with the final drive, as this cutaway shows. The V-8 engine has fuel injection, and ventilated disc brakes are used front and rear.

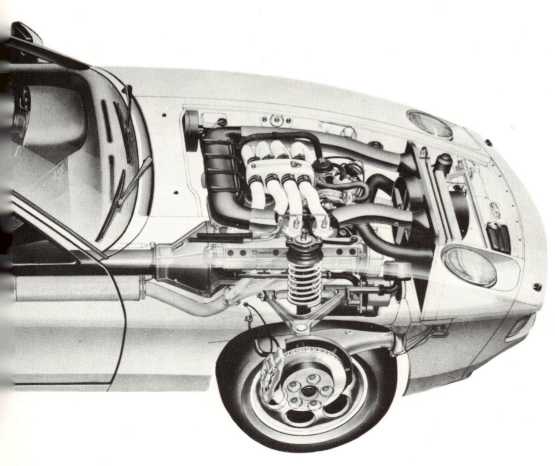

above
Aerodynamics is almost as much a matter of detail as overall shape. On the Porsche 928 the windows are not inside eddy-forming recesses in the body, and the lights are faired-in. Bumpers are plastic mouldings flush with the body shape.

Talbot-Lago

France gave a great deal to the sporting car. It had one of the world's first motor industries, and great cars flourished there in the Twenties and Thirties. Yet its politicians annihilated its luxury car makers, one by one, in the years following the war. Those manufacturers which had survived were penalized by a taxation system which imposed an annual fee of £100 (a large sum in 1946, equivalent to perhaps £1,000 thirty-five years later) on every car over 15 CV. Expensive cars brought income tax penalties, and under successive National Plans, manufacturers were unable to make up their own minds what cars to build; this was decided for them by bureaucrats '. . . in the national interest.'

The great cars, Delage, Delahaye, and Hotchkiss, were doomed. So were the classic coachbuilders such as Figoni et Falaschi, Chapron, and Saoutchik. Talbot was doomed too, but it struggled on longer than the others by virtue of success in Grand Prix racing and at Le Mans, together with the energy and driving force of Major Antony Lago, who had taken over the ailing firm in 1935.

Curiously, three of France's great automotive names, Bugatti, Gordini, and Lago, were all born in Italy. Lago was a Venetian who went to England following service in the Italian army in the First World War. He sold Isotta-Fraschinis in London before he joined Wilson, the preselector gearbox company, as technical director, and then Armstrong Siddeley, where he drove with enthusiasm for the works team in the 1932 Alpine Trials.

From there he went to the Sunbeam Talbot Darracq combine, an Anglo-French conglomerate already in financial trouble as a result of the trade depression and a marketing policy with a wasteful proliferation of makes and models. They quickly despatched the energetic Major Lago to France in an attempt to revive the French end of the business, the factory at Suresnes.

As a combine STD had little future; the Wolverhampton end was in poor shape and was soon to be taken over by the Rootes Group. Suresnes was better off on its own under Major Lago, who promptly resigned his English connections and took control. He found himself heir to all the French parts of the business, which included the Société Anonyme Darracq, Automobiles Talbot, and other famous names such as Clément-Bayard, Clément, Clément-Talbot, and so on.

It was the 3 litre K 78 Talbot-Darracq which formed the basis of the new programme. Chief engineer Walter Becchia developed a new cylinder head with cross-pushrods on the lines of the 328 BMW for the existing six cylinder engine, and production re-commenced. In 4 litre form, the engine was used as the basis for a racing car, and Lago's enthusiasm persuaded Rene Dreyfus to leave Ferrari and come and run the team.

Even bored out to 4½ litres, the Lago-Talbots (no firm order of precedence for the names was ever established) were no match for the Germans in Grand Prix racing, but they

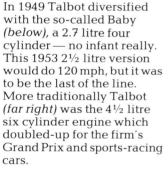

In 1949 Talbot diversified with the so-called Baby *(below)*, a 2.7 litre four cylinder — no infant really. This 1953 2½ litre version would do 120 mph, but it was to be the last of the line. More traditionally Talbot *(far right)* was the 4½ litre six cylinder engine which doubled-up for the firm's Grand Prix and sports-racing cars.

provided publicity for some splendid road cars with voluptuous French carrosserie, as well as a useful starting-block when operations resumed after the war. Indeed it was the ready supply of 4½ litre Talbots which enabled the post-war Formula A, as it was known, to be fixed at 1½ litres supercharged, and 4½ litres unsupercharged.

By then the engine had been rede-signed with two camshafts high up in the cylinder block and inclined valves worked by short pushrods, and was made suitable for both racing and road cars. Not only that, but the racing cars turned out to be adaptable not just for Grand Prix racing, but for sports car racing as well — in Italy Ferrari was following a similar line of development with his first 125s.

The production cars had 170 bhp and reached as many as 1,000 a year, the Grand Sport and Lago Record being built with striking coupe and saloon bodies. Racing successes included a sensational victory in the 1950 Le Mans, when Louis Rosier won almost single handed, a feat which Pierre Levegh tried to emulate two years later, his near success leading to a tragic drive with Mercedes-Benz in 1955.

But the penal taxation system took its toll of sales. Lago's reply was the Lago Baby, and later the Lago America, but production dropped to 100 cars a year and the racing team had to go. By 1954 the firm was forced to concentrate on the small model, a 4 cylinder GT coupe with 115 bhp, capable of 120 mph. Yet still there was no respite. Engine production was the next casualty, and Tony Lago was forced to buy 2.6 litre BMW V-8s, but by 1957 only two cars a week were being made, and the workshops were being hired out to other firms. In 1958 Lago sold out to Simca, and as a final crushing indignity the last Talbots were made with old side-valve Ford V-8s left over from the Simca Vedette. Lago died in 1960, the year production finally came to an end.

Postscript

Yet the name Talbot did survive.

It was a firm financed by the English Earl of Shrewsbury and Talbot which imported the first Clément-Bayard cars, and in 1903 this company re-formed to build Clément-Bayards in London. It was called Clement-Talbot Ltd, but dropped the Clement bit when it began making cars on its own account.

This firm was bought by the French Darracq company in 1919 to build Talbot cars in France, at Suresnes, the combined company becoming known as Sunbeam Talbot Darracq when the English Sunbeam firm was acquired. Lago bought the French part when the firm went under, and the Rootes Group bought the British. Automobiles Talbot was then acquired by Simca, and in time both Rootes and Simca were taken over by Chrysler.

The Talbot name was thus back under one roof, although it had not been used for many years. It was only when Peugeot SA took control of Chrysler Europe, and could no longer go on calling the cars Chryslers that Talbot, as not only the logical choice historically, but also because it proved popular with the marketing men, was selected for the new marque thus created.

In due course it even appeared once again on a sports car (see page 159).

LESSER LUMINARIES

Abarth

Carlo Abarth was an Austrian who specialized in taking Fiat components and giving them such a strong identity of their own that he could assemble them into another make of car altogether. He never attained production numbers like MG or the first Porsches, based on Morris and Volkswagen respectively, nor did he ever quite establish himself as an independent manufacturer, but Abarth cars gained a successful reputation in racing, and also as lightweight sports coupes on the road.

Abarth himself had worked on the Cisitalia Grand Prix project, and set up business in 1950 principally as a tuner of Fiats, although he did turn out a small

number of Abarth sports cars with Fiat 1100 engines, Porsche-type trailing arm ifs, and a number of Cisitalia sports car components. He was a clever publicist, and had some of them shown with dramatic-looking coachwork at international motor shows, giving Abarth cars a legitimacy which might otherwise have eluded them.

In 1955 his Zagato-bodied two seater had a bored-out 748cc Fiat 600 engine, developing 47 bhp, well over twice the standard car's output, giving it a top speed of over 100 mph. The later 850cc engine was provided with a twin-cam head by Abarth, and known as the Bialbero filled a high-revving, high-efficiency gap in the market not unlike that of the supercharged early MG Midgets.

By the early 1960s, the Abarth range was becoming rather more complicated,

Lowered suspension, lightweight wheels, and body paint distinguish this Abarth Fiat 595 from the standard Fiat 500 alongside.

Special-bodied Abarth coupes became the subject of motor show specials. This Pininfarina coupe has small conventional doors with frameless sliding windows which hinge upwards, complete with windscreen, to give access to the interior.

but it continued to be based either on tuned versions of Fiat saloons, or specially-built and distinctively-bodied coupes using Fiat-based engines. Most small Fiat saloons had equivalent Abarth versions, from the 500 producing 38 bhp, to a 1600 in an 850 body shell.

Abarth coupes included a 2 litre Simca Abarth of 200 bhp which was supposed to be able to do over 160 mph, but as the Sixties progressed, Abarths tended to become more racing and less sports. Their success, particularly on the track, made them the most conspicuous of all the tuners and special-builders who based their designs on Fiat parts.

As with Morris in the Thirties, then VW, Fiat, and Renault after the war, many useful sports cars began life in the components bins of large manufacturers. The trend persisted until the Seventies when major manufacturers, forced to achieve larger production volumes and more profit per unit, began discovering means of doing the job themselves.

Instead of allowing small firms to scavenge, and grow rich from the pickings, the big firms made racy coupes on their own account, leaving Abarth and their like to wither on the branch.

Allard

Racing on public roads was forbidden in Britain by nervous politicians and obstructive civil servants, resulting in a curiosity known as a 'trial'. This began as a contest to discover how far a car could climb a steep hill, then divided into contests to discover (a) how fast, and (b) how far they could climb a slippery hill. It was at this 'mud-plugging', as it was called, that Sydney Allard excelled, with a small car provided with strong torque from a 22 horse-power Ford V-8 engine.

Allard built a few replicas of his trials car, and after the war set up business in South London making extremely stylish open two seaters based on his experience and reputation in trials. They still used Ford V-8 engines, and their engineering was extremely straightforward, with a strong girder chassis and divided axle ifs. Yet they were good looking, if perhaps a little 'flashy', and had strong acceleration at a time when most British sports cars, based on pre-war standards of performance, did not.

Moreover, Allards did well in competition. With overhead valve conversions, or Cadillac and Chrysler V-8s as they became available, Allard won the 1952 Monte Carlo Rally, did well in sports car races such as Le Mans, and

established himself as an exporter of some merit. In the United States, the start-line punch and the deep throaty roar of a heavy V-8 was already the signal for heads to turn, after a fashion that the Cobra and many others would follow in years to come. The stark lines of the brutal J.2 Allard enhanced its appeal, even though protection from the weather was practically non-existent.

Allard saloons were rather grander affairs, but by 1953 the postwar boom was over. The days of premium prices for second-hand cars were gone; buyers were selective as choice returned, and cars built the traditional, expensive way needed replacing with new models. Small manufacturers had neither the experience nor the expertise to make the transition. Besides, Jaguar had brought out the XK 120 and the Mark VII. Everything else looked dated and indifferent value.

Allard's reply included a de Dion axle for the big saloon, now known as the Monte Carlo in celebration of its astonishing victory. In an effort to keep the American market alive he introduced two smaller cars, the Palm Beach models, with the new Consul and Zephyr four and six cylinder engines. But by 1956 production had dwindled almost to vanishing point. The final fling was a Mark II Palm Beach with an XK engine, but the customers clearly preferred the real thing, and only seven were made.

Racing in the streets, Elkhart Lake, Wisconsin, 14 September, 1951. Corwith Hamill (L-Type 4-seat Mercury Allard) passing David Felix's K-Type Cadillac Allard on the inside at Bank Corner at the start of the Novice's Race. Hamill won Class 2, and finished fourth overall. The onlookers, watching the Allards race a selection of XK 120 Jaguars, enjoyed a close view of the action.

Alpine

In the economy car idiom of the Fifties, Renaults were rear engined. The 760cc 4CV had been developed in the image of the Volkswagen. The Dauphine had been rear engined, and so had the Renault 8; it was the way small cars were, so far as the Continent of Europe was concerned. The vagaries of the handling were accepted because traction, roominess and ride were improved. Oversteer became a way of life.

Sports car derivatives had little choice but to follow the pattern. Automobiles Alpine started in 1955 with the Mille Miles, following a successful debut in the Mille Miglia. This had a glass fibre body, and it even looked a little like the 4CV, with its spider wheel hubs, on which the rims were bolted, and the air intake to the rear engine in the leading edges of the rear wings. Its builder Jean Rédéle entered the Mille Miglia again the following year, and the Alpine won its class, encouraging the development of open and closed models, as well as engine options of 845cc and 904cc.

Alpine was to Renault roughly what Abarth was to Fiat, and Porsche was (at first at any rate) to Volkswagen. The big manufacturers continued to smile on the minnows swimming in their wake. The nationalized Regie Renault had to be especially careful where racing was concerned, and it suited them very well to keep Alpine going with components and expertise. Racing successes would always reflect well on the bigger fish, while failures could always be blamed on the smaller.

When Renault wanted to compete at Le Mans, looking for class wins, it was Alpine they employed — a small, efficient organisation which could get on with the job.

Yet it was in rallies that the Alpine was to show its greatest potential.

Driving on loose or slippery surfaces demands above all that the driving wheels grip. Saabs, with their big wheels, good ground clearance and front wheel drive, were adept at it. And at the other end of the scale, so to speak, Alpines with their engines overhanging the back wheels were just as well suited. Rally drivers adopting the Scandinavian techniques of driving on special stages found the A110's oversteer matched their requirements exactly, and although it remained a tricky car for most other purposes, on snowy or loose-surfaced rallies it proved hard to beat.

Over the years Alpines became more and more powerful. The A310 for example, with a 1605cc Renault 16 engine modified by Gordini, had a top speed better than 130 mph. This was supplanted by the A310 V-6 of 2.7 litres,

Squatting on its negative-cambered rear wheels, the Alpine-Renault has a purposeful look; the A108 used an engine based on the older Dauphine, and the A110 used a developed version of the R.8.

using the co-operative Douvrin engine of 150 bhp, which made the car faster still.

Yet the extra speed and sophistication seemed to rest uneasily on the Alpine's shoulders. The highly-developed, thoroughly swervable little A110 that won the world rally championship of 1973 seemed an altogether tougher, more agile little car than the sleek 2+2 which replaced it.

Bizzarini

Giotto Bizzarini was nothing if not prolific.

From Alfa Romeo he went to Ferrari, where he laid out a long-secret small sports car project, eventually put into production in 1962 as the ASA, by Autocostruzioni Societa per Azioni. He was in charge of the development of one of the most famous Ferraris ever, the GTO. Then simultaneously, it would appear, he was a consultant to ISO, designing the Rivolta and Grifo, and working on the magnificent V-12 which powered every Lamborghini except the Urraco, meanwhile scheming up his own car in two versions, for road and track.

By any standards, it was a remarkable performance.

But just as writers are apt to have favourite phrases which they tend to

repeat, so some of Bizzarini's creations had a distinct similarity.

The sports-racing GT Strada employed a platform chassis with coil spring ifs and de Dion rear axle akin to the ISO Grifo of the same era. They even looked alike, but that was as much Bertone's fault as Bizzarini's — it also looked a bit like the Alfa Romeo Montreal because that was the fashion of the time.

It was less than a thoroughbred, however, in the tradition of the Modenese sports car as exemplified by Ferrari and Lamborghini. It had more in common with the Jensen of West Bromwich, in having its power supplied not by skilled indigenous metalworkers and craftsmen, but by Detroit.

American horse power proved just as strong as Italian, however, and it came a good deal cheaper. The Bizzarini's 5.3 litre GM V-8 gave it an urgent performance, a top speed of around 155 mph with acceleration to match, yet still customers turned out to be scarce. If they were prepared to pay the kind of money Bizzarini was asking, they were prepared to buy a Ferrari.

By 1965 Bizzarini was forced to turn his attention to something smaller, and showed a prototype based on a Fiat 1500 at the Turin motor show, but a year later he had abandoned this in favour of the Europa 1900, built in small numbers over the following two years.

The engine and gearbox turned out to be from the Opel Rekord, a worthy four cylinder 1,897cc unit with a cam-in-head arrangement producing over 100 bhp, giving the little fastback two seater coupe a lively turn of speed up to about 125 mph. A family resemblance to the big Bizzarini was achieved, and a reinforced glass fibre body shell kept the weight down to a commendable 1500 lbs. Yet still customers remained thin on the ground. There was not the demand for small expensive cars that there would be in the Seventies, when the price of petrol created a market for high-quality sports cars with a moderate consumption. Clients for costly cars still wanted them to look costly, and that meant big — yet bigness itself was not enough, as Bizzarini found with his Strada . . .

By 1969 it was apparent that the prolific Ing. Bizzarini had not discovered all the answers, and the little firm ceased making cars. Had it survived, perhaps things might have been different; an efficient, small, economical car such as the GT Europa might *just* have found a place for itself.

Chevrolet

The rationale behind the Chevrolet Corvette was not simply sales. Certainly, it was not an unprofitable operation for the mighty General Motors, and every V-8 engine sold was vital for the volume-dependent motor industry. Yet as Nash had already demonstrated in the Fifties, a sports car in the range was an invaluable promotional tool. It lent a certain excitement to the rest of the cars, to the dealer network, and to the employees making them to have representation at Le Mans. A competition programme improved motivation within the company, and enhanced its image without.

So, in a status-conscious country like America, owning a sports car became obligatory.

Chevrolet's bid for adventure was the Corvette. It was not an easy time for the American motor industry, with 1953-54 witnessing the formation of American Motors from a combination of Hudson and Nash, and the amalgamation of Packard and Studebaker, and the

Corvette was up against the new Ford Thunderbird.

The contrast between them was clear; the Chevrolet was a rather unlovely plastic-bodied two seater with a 3.86 litre six cylinder engine of 150 bhp, mounted in a modified production chassis frame with stiffened suspension. The Ford was good looking, with a 4¾ litre V-8 of 198 bhp, and a steel body. The Chevrolet was out of breath at 105 mph; the Ford would do 115.

Yet at under $4,000, the Chevrolet was the one that took off. Driven fast it had no brakes to speak of, but it would out-accelerate a Jaguar up to 60 mph, and out-corner any regular American car. The springing was less uncomfortable than imported sports cars, and the provision of automatic Powerglide transmission appealed to Americans to whom 'four-on-the-floor' was an unaccustomed complication.

By 1956, a V-8 engine of 4.3 litres and 180 bhp had been installed, and with the introduction of the Corvette Sting Ray in 1963, Europeans could no longer afford to be patronising. With a fuel injected engine of 5,360cc,

America's sports car. From 1973 the Chevrolet Corvette took on a slim-waisted look, with the fashionable rear spoiler added to the more traditional US shark-like beak. Rear window area was generous, and this model adopted the Porsche-style Targa top for open-air motoring.

below
The 1958 Corvette.

developing 360 bhp (gross), and independent rear suspension, it was a match for any European car. The chassis was still a stout box-section affair, and the well-finished body was still made of glass reinforced plastic, but now it had good proportions and striking lines with foldaway headlights. A Borg Warner manual gearbox was available, and the Sting Ray would do 145 mph and handle well in the dry at least; it needed European tyres to do well in the wet.

It still had drum brakes, with sintered metallic linings in an effort to tame the immense performance, and the steering was not as precise as drivers more accustomed to European

standards expected. Yet the independent rear suspension, which resembled the E-Type Jaguar's in some respects, put the Corvette firmly into the top league for ride and handling; its price moreover was still astonishingly low.

With re-styling and facelifting, and engines up to 7 litres, the Corvette went on to become one of the world's longest-running sports cars. Its stable-mates Camaro and Cougar, or the smaller Monza 2+2, were never quite in the same sporting idiom; even the Pontiac Firebird never captured the hearts and minds of the traditional sports car buffs the way the Corvette did, despite strong racing affiliations.

The first hand-made production Chevrolet Corvette drives off the assembly line in Flint, Michigan on 30 June, 1953.

The completely re-styled 1963 Corvette with hardtop.

Cisitalia

Every constellation has its share of stars which burn brilliantly but briefly. Cisitalia was one.

Commendatore Piero Dusio was wealthy, well-connected, and dedicated to motor racing. He had been Italy's champion amateur driver before the war with a blown 2.5 litre Alfa Romeo, and afterwards saw his chance to build small sports and racing cars in production quantities. Using plenty of readily available standard parts, he reasoned, he would have the market almost to himself.

He got Fiat's influential designer Dante Giacosa to draw up plans for a tubular-framed chassis which could take Fiat suspension and 1100 engines. The car looked the part, and Dusio had plans for a sort of Formula Cisitalia along the lines later realized as Formula Ford, Formula Vee, or Formula Renault. He even persuaded the legendary Nuvolari to drive a two-seater version of the car in the 1947 Mille Miglia, which he led until rain penetrated the electrical system, forcing him out.

Encouraged, Dusio went into Grand Prix racing in the biggest possible way, engaging the Porsche design office, which had been exiled to Gmünd in Austria, to design him a car. This was the astonishingly prophetic flat-twelve four-wheel-drive Cisitalia-Porsche 360. A formidable team of engineers worked on the project, including the Porsches father and son, Karl Rabe, Eberan von Eberhorst, and Carlo Abarth, until the money ran out, and Dusio had to export the whole scheme to find sponsorship from Juan Peron, the Argentine dictator, in an abortive attempt to complete it.

The design remains the racing car which was probably ahead of its time by the biggest margin in history.

So far as the story of the sports car was concerned, the Cisitalia was almost equally significant. Once again, this was not owing to the inventiveness of Dusio so much as to the genius he engaged for the job.

Battista Farina, nicknamed Pininfarina, left the Stabilimenti Farina in 1930 to found his own car body factory and styling studio in Turin. Amongst his pioneering designs were developments of the inclined windscreen and the horizontal radiator intake. His cars aimed to integrate engineering and art after the model of Walter Gropius and the Bauhaus school. In 1947 he created

Pininfarina's prophetic 1947 Cisitalia coupe civilized the pre-war Le Mans streamliners, and found echoes on both sides of the Atlantic. A later version had two porthole-style air outlets just aft of the front wheel arch, mercilessly copied in the United States.

the Cisitalia coupe, which came to represent the turning-point of car style in the postwar world.

What Pininfarina had done was amalgamate the new aerodynamic regime with something habitable, practical, manufacturable, and above all saleable. The 1947 Cisitalia 202 was exhibited at the Museum of Modern Art in New York as an example of moving sculpture. Its lines were soon echoed by manufacturers as diverse as Buick and Lancia; its full-width two door fastback body set a pattern that was followed for the next 35 years and more.

The Cisitalia owed much to the pre-war racing coupes, notably the 8C2900B Alfa Romeo which so nearly won Le Mans in 1938. This body by Touring of Milan never gained the recognition it deserved. Pininfarina refined and added subtle touches, such as the vestigial rear wing line which lightened it and relieved the slab-sided appearance.

So far as Cisitalia was concerned, however, that was very nearly the end of the road. Dusio came back from Argentina after failing to get his Grand Prix project off the ground in a country whose engineers were simply not up to the task of taking over where Porsche, von Eberhorst, and Abarth had left off. He continued making sports cars on and off into the Sixties, but by then the spark of accomplishment had gone, the capability grown cold. The final Cisitalias were warmed-up versions of the Fiat 600, and unremarkable by any standards.

Front view of the 1947 Cisitalia.

Cooper

Charles and John Cooper were a father and son from Surbiton in Surrey, whose instinct for engineering and facility as copiers took them into the highest ranks of racing and sports car builders. They not only won the world motor racing championships twice over but achieved a design revolution.

In the stringent economic circumstances which followed the war, cut-price schemes for motor racing abounded. Most of them involved taking components from standard cars and making them appear like the racing cars with which enthusiasts were familiar. In Britain the recreation of building hill-climb specials produced a class of car which was more radical.

This was the 500cc engined single-seater which mounted motor-cycle units behind the driver, with transmission to the rear wheels by means of gearbox and chain. It was a simple four-wheeled motorcycle with the driver sitting in it instead of astride it, and the absence of a differential gear was excused on the grounds of expense.

The Coopers took to the new Formula 3, as it became known, like ducks to water. They cobbled up cars with Fiat 500 front suspension front *and* rear; transverse leaf and wishbone springing giving such good road holding that they were virtually unbeatable.

When they diversified into sports cars, the Coopers, inventive though they were, tended to stick to what they knew. Thus their first were no more than up-rated versions of their 500 chassis, with bigger engines, water-cooling, and a proper differential. The transverse leaf spring independent suspension remained, just as it did on their racing cars, and it was only with the Mark 2 version of the extremely powerful Cooper-Bristol that they went so far as a tubular chassis along Cisitalia lines.

Yet the small MG-engined sports cars with which Cooper went into limited production in 1950 still had what were basically re-worked Fiat 500 frames. They were stark open two-seaters with cycle-type wings and no weather protection at all.

Later Cooper sports cars had diverse engines such as Maserati and Jaguar, but they were mostly limited production runs intended for racing. Indeed it was Cooper who led racing design into the mid-engined configuration with the 'centre seat' Cooper Climax.

Cunningham

It was not given to many men to create their very own make of sports car — as a hobby.

Briggs Swift Cunningham, however, was wealthy enough to join that exclusive company to whom the description 'sportsmen' would be applied. Yachting for the America's Cup and competing in the great 24 Hours race at Le Mans came easily to Cunningham, who was eventually to open his famous motor museum at Costa Mesa, California, after earning great fame and affection among European sports car enthusiasts.

Cunningham first wiped the smile from their faces in 1950, by entering two Cadillacs at Le Mans; one a huge, barge-like two seater, the other a stock 61 sedan, tuned, but a good deal closer to standard trim than most of the other cars in the race. Competing against the best of the world's sports cars, the sedan finished 10th and the clumsy two seater 11th, despite an accident which made the tank-like body uglier still.

For 1961 Cunningham built three special two-seaters with tubular frames, Chrysler engines, de Dion rear axles, and wide, open two-seater bodies. This was the C-2R, and two cars crashed, but the third held second place for nearly five hours before dropping back through engine and transmission trouble to finish 18th.

To comply with Le Mans regulations, the C-3 Cunningham was put into production — a minimum of 25 cars was specified — and they were based closely on the Le Mans cars, with a Chrysler live rear axle instead of de Dion, and a German ZF four speed gearbox with semi-automatic change. The imposing GT bodywork was designed by Michelotti and made by Vignale, and the closed version sold for $10,000 while an open version was available for $11,000.

The definitive Cunningham, however, was developed for the 1952 race. The C-4R had rather more graceful lines but was still massive by European standards. Despite its looks it was 1,000 lbs lighter and a team of three, two open cars and one coupe, acquitted themselves well. Briggs Cunningham himself drove for 20 hours out of the 24, to finish 4th. Also in 1953 Cunninghams won the Sebring 12 Hours, one of a number of convincing wins the make scored in the United States.

Perseverance paid off at Le Mans, when the C-5 finished 3rd in 1953 and the C-4R which came 3rd and 5th in 1954, but even Cunningham's millions were not to be spent year after year in pursuit of victory; they had been well invested already in that sporting ambassadorial role which so many Americans (like Dan Gurney and Mario Andretti to come) filled with such credit.

Cunningham's happy team probably did more for United States prestige in Europe than many a professional diplomat. The cars were probably too big and too generous to compete with the newcomers such as the C and D-Type Jaguars, or the super-efficient Mercedes-Benz. Yet they showed the way for America to enter the hitherto exclusive sports-racing world — and showed there was a commercial harvest in it waiting to be reaped.

After a 20-hour drive, Briggs Cunningham finished fourth in the 1952 Le Mans race. The open C-4R was beaten by two 300 SL Mercedes-Benz and a Nash-Healey.

D-B and René Bonnet

Duplication or duplicity? The René Bonnet team at Le Mans in 1964 unloaded two identical number 60s (even the registration numbers were the same) presumably to have a full spares back-up in the event of anything going wrong. They had won the Index of Thermal Efficiency in 1963, so were not leaving anything to chance. The Index went to Alpine-Renault however, their best result was seventh in the formula-based award, and all three *Aérodjets* were out of the race after six hours.

Next to Daimler-Benz, Panhard was the oldest and most respected name in motoring. Yet a more unlikely basis for a sports car would be hard to find. Horizontally opposed twin cylinder engines were fine for the penal taxation system established by the French after the war, but they were hardly the stuff for exciting driving.

Charles Deutsch and René Bonnet, however, knew how to make the best of the most unpromising material. They had started making specials based on 11 CV front wheel drive Citroens in 1938.

The flat-twin Dyna Panhard saloon came out in 1946 with 610cc and 28 bhp, and it was not until 1950 that this developed to 750cc and a dizzy 32 bhp. The 1953 sports version boasted no less than 38 bhp. In an effort to give these

somewhat dreary little cars some sort of competition to win, the French invented the Index of Performance at Le Mans, which Dyna Panhards entered by the Ecurie Monopole won every year from 1950 to 1953.

Deutsch and Bonnet saw their chance, and brought out a sports version of the Dyna Panhard, alloy-bodied at first, then, from 1955, in a rather bulgy glass fibre. At Le Mans they took over where the Monopoles left off, winning the Index of Performance in 1954, 1956, 1959, 1960, and 1961. They even made an attempt to take part in the 1954 Grand Prix Formula, with a 750cc supercharged car against the 2½ litre unsupercharged cars, but despite a handsome reputation for getting a lot out of a little, no Formula 1 car ever appeared.

One of their production cars did have a supercharger, however, an optional belt-driven affair supposed to encourage the Monomills, which was an early attempt at a one-design Formula for cheap single-seater racing.

It was not until the partnership was broken up in 1961 that a really useful contribution was made to the history of the French sports car. Deutsch went to Panhard as technical adviser, but Bonnet carried on in the works at Champigny-sur-Marne to make the interesting Matra Bonnet Djet.

Instead of the front-wheel-drive of the D-B era, the new René Bonnet was mid-engined with rear wheel drive. Matra came in after the design had been crystallized by Bonnet, representing the first excursion into motor racing by the French missile and aerospace concern — a connection which was to be far-reaching.

Instead of using Panhard components as the basis for the Djet, Bonnet had gone to Renault, but unlike the Alpine, the Bonnet was mid-engined, and not rear-engined. Both cars used mechanical components from the Renault 8, in the case of the Bonnet with the engine and transaxle turned through 190°.

Matra, however, had more grandiose plans than they could bring to fruition in the little Bonnet works. Once the lessons of the backbone frame and plastic body were absorbed, they proceeded to close down their acquisition, and the last Bonnet was built in 1968. Matra had their eye on single-seater racing, and the production of a mid-engined coupe in a new factory at Romorantin — the Matra M530A (see page 151).

Delahaye and Delage

It was 1934 when the makers of a long line of rather staid, formal saloons suddenly turned their hand to sports cars. Delahaye had not long rid themselves of wooden wheels and side valves when they quite unexpectedly brought out the Superluxe, with a 3.2 litre six cylinder ohv engine, transverse leaf independent front suspension, and low, attractive lines.

An improved version with 120 bhp became the famous Type 135 which, in competition form, gave 160 bhp and over 115 mph. To complete the transformation, dreary old Delahaye went racing and began equipping their road cars with Cotal electro-magnetic gearboxes. Delahayes came 5th at Le Mans in 1935, 2nd, 3rd, 4th, and 5th in the 1936 French sports car Grand Prix, 2nd at Le Mans in 1937, and 1st, 3rd and 4th in 1938. They won the 1937 and 1939 Monte Carlo Rallies, bought the Delage company, and brought out a V-12 which came 4th in the Mille Miglia, and on one occasion, with a Grand Prix car, even beat the mighty Mercedes-Benz team.

Accordingly, Delahaye got off to a good start when peace broke out in 1945. Commencing production the following year with the 135, now with 130 bhp, they won the Monte again in 1951, although the cars were now less sporting than they had been. A new model, the 4½ litre Type 175, came out in 1948 with a top speed of over 100 mph and hydraulic brakes. They tried another new car, the 235, with fashionable full-width bodywork; Delage re-introduced their pre-war 3 litre D.6, and although there was no sports Delahaye in the catalogue, one ran at Le Mans in 1949 and finished 2nd behind Lord Selsdon's Ferrari.

Sadly, the penal French taxation system was taking its toll. Combined sales of Delahayes and Delages dropped from 483 in 1950 to only 77 in 1951. A four-wheel-drive Jeep-style vehicle failed to revive the firm's fortunes, and it was forced into an amalgamation with Hotchkiss, itself in difficulties. The combine made trucks instead, and Delahaye headed, along with many other famous French makes of car, into oblivion.

Delahaye with bodywork by Figoni et Falaschi built for the Maharaja of Mysore.

de Tomaso

Something between a GT 40 and a Lamborghini Miura to look at, the De Tomaso Pantera outperformed them both in the market place.

The route was somewhat circuitous, but a meeting of the minds was eventually achieved between the traditional, craft-inclined Modenese, and the production-dependent masters of Michigan. Despite a car building philosophy separated by more than the yawning Atlantic, Alessandro de Tomaso was able to bring together such diverse elements as the Ford Motor Company of America, Maserati, Ghia, and the Italian Government.

It had not been easy for the world to take de Tomaso seriously. An Argentinian racing driver of no great reputation, he embarked on a number of spectacular projects in the late Fifties which were long on promises, but short on fulfilment. He lent his name to a Grand Prix car which Frank Williams ran, and built a variety of prototype road cars of variable distinction. These included the Vallelunga with a Cortina engine in the back, of which about 50 were actually made.

De Tomaso's master stroke was buying Ghia just as the coachbuilding industry was going into decline, and putting a 4.7 litre V-8 into the Vallelunga. Styled by Ghia, and with a ZF five speed gearbox in a chassis which used a pressed steel backbone frame and tubular sub-frames, the Mangusta was a spectacular production for 1966. Like some other de Tomaso brainwaves of course, it looked better than it went, and with 68 per cent of the weight on the back wheels, the handling was problematical, particularly in the wet. Large-section rear tyres were a palliative, but the car was too close to being a racer, and not close enough to being a road car to be a success at either.

Redemption was at hand however in the shape of Ford, who relieved de Tomaso of Ghia, and took a hand in a re-design of the Mangusta. It reappeared at the 1970 New York motor show as the Pantera, now a pressed steel monocoque which would be put into production for Ford to sell in North America through their Lincoln-Mercury dealers. A severely stock 5.8 litre V-8 gave the Pantera even more speed — up to 160 mph — and the weight distribution was improved, with only 58 per cent on the back wheels. The tyres were still different sizes, but there was more accommodation than before. Air conditioning ensured its appeal to luxury buyers who may have valued its striking appearance and GT 40 resemblance, with its racing chisel nose, rather more than its road performance in any case.

By supercar standards, the Pantera was a high flyer, with more than 4,000 made and sold.

It represented the legitimization of de Tomaso, who widened his scope of operations in 1972 with the four-door Deauville, a front-engined saloon, followed quickly by the Longchamps, much the same but shorter, with two doors.

As with so many specialist manufacturers however, de Tomaso was affected by the oil crisis, and the Ford relationship was downgraded. But neighbouring Maserati were feeling the pinch even more, and de Tomaso took the opportunity of amalgamating with the help of Government finance, and rationalizing the model lines. This meant exchanging the Ford V-8 for a Maserati V-8 in the Longchamps, and re-launching it as a Maserati Kyalami. De Tomaso also resuscitated the long-dead Quattroporte, and re-launched it as well, with a similar kinship to the Deauville.

Fiat

If only Fiat had persevered with models such as the 8V of 1952-54, they might have aspired to the Grand Marques instead of skulking here amongst the Lesser Luminaries. Faced with the dilemma which confronts volume manufacturers from time to time over a highly specialized product which can at best be a gamble, they opted out. They chose to modify some of their volume models on the one hand, and find common cause with Ferrari on the other.

The 8V was conceived in a world emerging from the war, still crisis-laden, but full of hope nonetheless. In Germany Mercedes-Benz were building their 300 SLs, in Britain Jaguar were making the C-Type. Fiat wanted to uphold Italian prestige in a way that even traditional sports car manufacturers were not considered up to. The proposition, nurtured from the Mercedes-Benz and Auto Union days of the Thirties, was that automotive technology had reached the point where only large manufacturers with elaborate facilities were capable of producing great cars.

Accordingly, Fiat embarked on a tubular chassis, and a V-8 with the cylinders unusually disposed at 70° in order to fit in a narrow engine space. It was a real flight of fancy for one of the largest and most influential motor manufacturers in Europe. Engineers, it was argued, must be given the opportunity to build such a car in order to learn how to make the mass-transit 600s and 1100s better — yet another rationale for the sports car.

It was one of the first to have the body shape decided in the wind tunnel, and only a few suspension components bore any similarity to anything made for Fiat's vast and extremely successful range of cars. The 8V was unique.

If the engine had been more amenable to tuning (it had rather small valves) it might have been seen in racing, but 130 bhp was about its limit, and although it won the Italian 2 litre championship in 1954, it was not really man enough to compete in the big league at Le Mans. Only 114 were ever built, some with bodies by Ghia or Zagato. Weight was just under a ton, and top speed around 125 mph.

After this Fiat recognized the limitations of a sports car programme, conceding that for them to be involved meant tackling it wholeheartedly.

Bored-out version of the OSCA-designed twin cam 1500, the Fiat 1600S Cabriolet had 100 bhp in 1963-66, when it had to make way for the 124 sports versions.

Only 114 Fiat 8Vs were ever built. The lightweight production fast-back coupe was a racing-style shell built without much thought for comfort or quietness.

127

By Fiat out of Ferrari, the Fiat Dino was an ungainly and, as it turned out, a sickly infant. This 1966 Fiat Dino was further proof that sports cars can often be perfectly ordinary marques driven up-market, but the converse is not always a success.

Failures were very public, and it was easier to farm out the sporting side to Abarth and blame them when things went wrong. Fiat could still accept the credit for success.

It was 1961 before they made anything else resembling a sports car. This was the 2300S, really no more than a two door fastback coupe on the excellent 2.3 litre six cylinder saloon floor pan, but it had the looks and sounds of a Ferrari and did a respectable 120 mph.

The 1200 and 1600 models were made as sporty coupes and open two seaters, as were the lively 850s with their pretty bodies by Bertone and their rear engines. More significant was the 1600S, which had a twin-cam engine designed by OSCA, but made by Fiat. It ran into stiff opposition in Italy from Alfa Romeo in the middle Sixties and was never a great commercial success.

The 124 Sport Spider on the other hand rivalled the MGB as one of the world's longest-running sports cars. Even after the 124 saloon from which it was derived ceased production, the open two-seater carried on for the United States market. Like the MG it suffered '5 mph' bumpers, but the twin-cam four cylinder with which it made its debut at the Turin show of 1966 was a little more able to cope with the extra weight. A lightweight Abarth version enjoyed a successful rally career with a 16-valve head.

Once Ford's overtures had been firmly rejected in 1962, Fiat went into partnership with Ferrari instead. The factory at Maranello was enlarged, and while Ferrari retained control of the racing department, Fiat effectively took control of road cars.

The first fruit of the arrangement appeared in 1966, when the Dinos were announced. Ferrari had already shown a prototype with the V-6, 65° engine, known as the Dino and made in a variety

The 1972 Fiat 124 Sport Rally, Italy's somewhat more effective answer to the MGB. Matt black bonnet was a passing fashion when rally drivers adopted it to reduce reflections at night.

of sizes between 1½ and 2½ litres, and various states of tune from Grand Prix downwards.

Ferrari Dinos were mid-engined, but Fiat Dinos, made in Maranello, labelled as Fiats and sold through the Fiat dealer network, were front-engined. Open and closed models, with clean-lined bodies (Bertone for the coupe, Pininfarina for the more voluptuous open Spider) had five speed gearboxes and live rear axles, appearing for the first time at the Geneva motor show in the spring of 1967.

The cars were undeniably handsome, and handled well, yet somehow the arrangement never quite worked out. It may have been something to do with the humble connotations of their Fiat badges, even though the engineering was undeniably Ferrari. Premium

Bertone-bodied rear-engined Fiat 850 tried to make a diminutive car look longer by building in rather a lot of overhang front and rear.

The mid-engine reaches the bargain market. Fiat may not have intended to get into the popular sports car business at all, but they were unable to resist the charm and style of the Bertone-inspired X1/9. Large numbers of buyers shared their enthusiasm for the pert and pretty replica of the big-engined racers of Le Mans and elsewhere.

prices seemed to demand something more up-market for commercial success.

In strong contrast to the philosophy which resulted in the 8V — that large resources and armies of technicians were necessary for the successful gestation of a modern sports car — the X1/9 was the result of a small team working alone. The Bertone design office dreamed up a mid-engined coupe with a Fiat 128 engine and transmission to replace the rear-engined 850s on which much of their livelihood had depended. They sold the notion to Fiat, and the result was one of the best small sports cars of the age.

The X1/9 was not only a styling triumph, it handled superbly, and in stark contrast to the plain VW-Porsche

914 it had room for luggage as well. Like the 914 there was little space left over once the occupants were installed, but for speed and economy (108 mph and 30 mpg) it fulfilled the role which MG left vacant when they phased out the Midget and replaced it with nothing. The X1/9, using standard components to best advantage, looked the part, and behaved in just the way the perceptive Kimber would have liked had he lived a generation later. Furthermore, the inventive Bertone demonstrated that the technology of the motor car had not advanced so far into the laser and microchip age that a small, well-knit team of commercially-motivated and talented people was no longer capable of producing a brilliant sporting car.

Ford

The GT 40 alone was a landmark in the evolution of the sports car, but Ford had a good deal more to say about the subject than that. In America there were the Thunderbird and the Mustang, in Europe the Lotus-Cortina, the RS Escort, and the Capri.

Nothing illustrates the blurred definition of a sports car more than the diversity of the Fords which qualify. The Thunderbird, for example, was only a sports car during its youth. Not all models of the Mustang could be considered sports cars. And the humility of some Capris only served to illustrate the skill of the marketing men, who even if they could not make every model a silk purse, at least managed to play down some of the sow's ears.

The first clean-limbed Thunderbirds appeared in 1954, and Europeans, accustomed to smaller, more tightly-knit cars, had to acknowledge a grudging admiration for their good proportions and lusty acceleration — even with automatic transmission. Who, within the bastions of sports car tradition, could guess that in time Porsche would equip their leading models with automatic, and Jaguar would come not even to offer the option of a manual in the XJS?

Surprisingly, Thunderbirds put on weight, grew bigger after only three seasons, and America had to wait until 1964 before Ford repeated their sporting experiment. This time they did not call it a sports car.

The inventiveness of people who sell cars knows no bounds. For years manufacturers had followed a pattern; the four-door sedan was the top seller — the

The speediest Mustang, with the 335bhp, 7,013cc Cobra Jet Ram Air engine, 'through the bonnet' air scoop, body side tape stripe, and rear spoiler. Yet the Mach 1 was not all talk; the acceleration was formidable, even if the roadholding and braking left a certain amount to be desired.

two-door could be made cheaper; it sold fewer, so it was priced cheaper.

Now somebody stood the idea on its head. If the two-door could be made to have special appeal, it could be sold *dearer*, and if the mechanical parts were the same and only the body a little different, the mark-up would be correspondingly bigger. As a ploy for profit enhancement, it was a stroke of genius.

The result was the Mustang. It used the chassis and engine of other Fords, principally Falcon, together with an individually-styled two-door body, and it was called a 'personal car'. No longer the down-market cheap car, the two-door was promoted to the premium bracket. The idea took off with soaring sales, 400,000 within the first twelve months, and the first million by 1966. Tuners such as Shelby made it faster, and enhancements, such as the Mach 1,

that ultimate virility symbol, soon followed.

Alas, Mustang the muscle-car became another casualty of the Arab oil embargo and the 1973 Israeli war; a jittery America emasculated it and shrunk it, weighed it down with fenders and protectionism. A symbol of the Sixties slipped from view.

The differences between the American and European markets were shown in the differences between the Mustang and the Capri. Yet the principle remained the same. Using the Cortina for a basis, a two-door model could be sold at a premium, raising volume, enhancing the image, capturing a young market which would continue buying Ford. The customers knew they were buying sporting style rather than sporting performance. There were few illusions about the Capri, yet it was the basis of a sporting car, as it could

overleaf
Sports cars, by definition, included cars used for sport. This Ford Capri competed in the Spa 24 Hours race, which took the place, in many senses, of Le Mans as the premier long-distance event for cars which at least resembled production cars. Driven by Gordon Spice and Teddy Pilette, the resemblance is more than superficial in this case, although many so-called production cars were really nothing of the sort.

Ford of America's stroke of genius. The Mustang created a whole new market for what Ford called a 'personal car', something between a sports car and a family coupe which proved one of the American industry's most profitable models. The 1965 Mark 1.

opposite
A Ford Escort Twin Cam jumps for joy during testing of a new sump shield at Bagshot in preparation for the 1969 rally season. Roger Clark, whose successes in Ford Escorts included two outright wins in the RAC Rally, was the driver on this occasion.

demonstrate in races against the well-bred might of BMW. Capris could hold their own — once the regulations gave them a little elbow room and allowed them to compete on favourable terms.

No such concessions were needed for the other European sporting Fords. Even in a huge corporation individuals could influence events disproportionately. Walter Hayes joined Ford of Britain as Head of Public Affairs, and immediately saw the value of taking part in competition. A later product of Hayes' flair for capturing the public's imagination would be the Ford-Cosworth Grand Prix engine — the most successful racing engine ever. But in 1963, hot on the heels of the first Cortina, came the Lotus-Cortina.

The idea was to have limited production of these special Cortinas carried out by Lotus, with their suspension suitably modfied to make them handle better, and the Lotus Twin Cam engine designed by Harry Mundy to make them faster. With Walter Hassan, Mundy had conceived the brilliant series of Coventry-Climax racing engines, and would later collaborate with Hassan again on the V-12 Jaguar.

The Lotus-Cortina illustrated the difference between handling and road holding. On a racing circuit, it would wave one front wheel in the air on corners, yet remain firmly under control, the rear wheels held in check by an A-frame designed by Colin Chapman. But like so many products carrying the Lotus badge at the time, reliability was suspect. By 1966 Ford regained control

of production, and called it simply the Cortina Twin Cam. In any case, they abandoned the essentially Lotus part, the modified suspension, in favour of a leaf-sprung rear which was more dependable but did not provide as much cornering power. Later cars were also more refined and quieter.

The Lotus-Cortina was essentially a race-bred car, but the Escort gained its spurs in rallies. And while the Twin Cam engine was effective enough, in their pursuit of the sublime Ford decided to go further up the performance gradient.

When Georges Boillot, Jules Goux and Paul Zuccarelli stood round the drawing board of 26-year-old Ernest Henry, laying plans for the 1912 Grand Prix Peugeot engine, they were evolving the classic cylinder head pattern of two overhead camshafts operating the valves directly. It was efficient, and became the established layout for racing engines, but mostly with two valves per cylinder. The Peugeot had four, and when Ford went in search of something better than the Mundy Twin Cam, they came up with the Cosworth-designed BDA — with four valves per cylinder.

The RS (for Racing Sport, or *Rennsport* — it was made in Germany as well as Britain) 1600 and later 2000 Escorts had all the speed and handling of a sports car with the accommodation of an ordinary saloon. They were never as quiet of course, and they were more turbulent over bumps, but they proved far more effective than any so-called sports car in the rough and tumble of

Gordon-Keeble

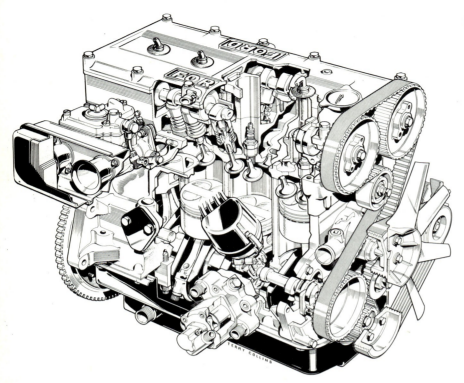

Developed by Cosworth, in many respects resembling one-half of the DFV Formula 1 engine, but with the camshafts driven by toothed belt instead of gears, the RS 1600 was one of a family generation of Ford and Cosworth four-valve-per-cylinder engines which applied racing practice to road-going sporting cars.

opposite
A fraction under three per cent of the entire production of the famous Anglo-American hybrid Gordon-Keeble, which scored heavily on quality, but not sufficiently on sales to support itself. The body style is early Giugiaro, the engine a robust V-8, but the innate conservatism of the quality buyer preferred better-known makes with established reputations.

off-road sporting events. The bodies were strengthened, for in order to win the 1979 world rally championship, the RAC Rally of Great Britain eight years in a row and the London-Mexico World Cup Rally, the relatively cheaply-made little cars had to be prevented from literally coming apart at the seams through being pounded over rocks and potholes at high speeds.

Ford may not exactly have set out to make sports cars, but if you include in the definition cars which did well in sport, they must be counted. More than almost any other make except perhaps the Mini, European Fords were responsible for the eclipse of the open two-seater as the acme of sporting car perfection. They convinced the most die-hard that speed, acceleration and good behaviour on corners were obtainable without draughts or cramped seating. Fords often had the advantage of *not* attracting attention when it was unwelcome, for example from police to some of whom the very sight of an MG meant reaching for stopwatch and notebook. The title 'sports' also worried insurance companies although they soon grasped the significance of RS or Twin Cam and loaded premiums accordingly.

For Ford, the motor sporting connection proved durable and successful, proving beyond doubt that making sports cars need not be ephemeral, trivial, extravagant, or costly.

The idea of a big American engine in a European-style chassis was not exactly new in 1964. Since the war Allards had had Chrysler and Cadillac V-8s, and Healey took the idea further by using a Nash engine in a car with a not unelegant body by Pininfarina.

Thus was the slightly cut-price Italianate GT born. The complexity and expense of the exquisite V-12s and V-8s from Ferrari, Lamborghini and Maserati were rejected; but it was hoped that with equally good roadholding and handling, and just as much sense of style, you could achieve much the same effect with a simple V-8 from the United States.

The Peerless, later the Warwick GT, was a low-volume specialist British GT car which competed with the Triumph TR4 and Austin-Healey 100/6 in 1960-62. It had a tubular chassis platform and a glass reinforced plastic body. Most had Triumph TR engines, but a few were made with the interesting light-alloy Buick V-8 later taken up by Rover.

Peerless did not survive as a company, but John Gordon and Jim Keeble, who had worked in it, set up on their own afterwards to design a new car with a Chevrolet V-8 engine, de Dion rear suspension, and an extremely elegant body designed by Bertone. The prototype was given an enthusiastic reception as the first big GT car made in Britain capable of mounting a challenge to the Italians on almost every score. It looked good, it handled well, and it was fast and well finished.

The foundations of the company making it were insecure, however, and there were delays in getting production going. Even when it did, making small numbers of cars turned out to be unprofitable, and one of the company's dealers had to mount a rescue operation and set up a new factory. But this was not enough, and the firm folded after making just one short of a hundred cars.

Against competition from Jaguar and Jensen, the Gordon-Keeble stood little chance. Prejudice lingered over its plastic body — Jensen went over to a steel body — and although it did 135 mph and looked every inch a powerful prestige car, it had no pedigree, and to such a discriminating clientele good breeding, it seemed, was vital.

Healey and Austin-Healey

Like many individuals who gave their names to cars, Donald Healey was a skilled publicist. He had been a competition driver and Technical Director of Triumph before the war, his exploits including outright victory in the 1931 Monte Carlo Rally, and six Alpine Cups. Afterwards, with Triumph in receivership, he set out to make cars on his own account in a small factory at The Cape, Warwick, using engines from Riley, for whom he had worked before joining Triumph.

Like Allard in Britain and Dusio in Italy, Healey seized his opportunites in a postwar world hungry for cars of almost any sort, and altogether starved of sports cars. Along with AC Sampietro, in October 1946 he brought out almost the first wholly new design to appear anywhere. The fine four cylinder, high camshaft engines made the hand-built Healeys amongst the fastest cars catalogued in Britain, and their repu-

tation was enhanced by some well-publicized achievements in the Mille Miglia. By virtue of their sturdy chassis frame, and rather extravagantly engineered trailing link ifs and well-located coil-sprung rear axle, the Healeys handled well too.

The somewhat bulbous styling was well received, and Donald Healey, like many another British manufacturer, set off for America. In order to buy scarce raw materials, he had to convince the authorities that he was in the export business.

Although only 105 were ever made, the most significant Healey was the Silverstone. Produced in 1949-50 primarily for competition, it was the pre-war style stripped-down two-seater brought up to date, with cycle-type wings and headlamps concealed behind the diamond-shaped grille. It was light, fast and, in the best tradition of the sporting car, it could be driven to the circuit and be instantly ready for racing.

The essential difference between Healey and Allard was that when the market changed, Allard failed to adapt, while Healey had set up a relationship with the Nash-Kelvinator Corporation

Bulbous style of the times. The start of the 1948 Mille Miglia with Donald Healey at the wheel of a Healey Westland Roadster, along with son Geoffrey. They finished ninth overall, and second in the unlimited sports car class.

The Austin-Healey 3000 Mark III introduced in March 1962 reverted to a twin-carburettor engine. The body was improved with winding windows and a convertible-style hood, yet the basic shape was unchanged from the 100/6 of 1956, the first of the six-cylinder models. The fine proportions of the big Healey made it one of the most graceful sports cars ever.

to build a sports car using their 3.8 litre six cylinder engine. The Nash-Healey was sold through Nash's dealer network, in small numbers admittedly, but it created interest and what the trade calls showroom traffic, and helped to sell the rest of the range.

Only 404 Nash-Healeys were made, but they established the principle of co-operation with a big manufacturer which led to the creation of one of the best-looking and best-loved sports cars ever, the Austin-Healey 100.

The engine and major mechanical units came from Austin's unlovely A90, and Healey wrapped them in the curvaceous envelope that was to survive from the introduction of the four-speed gearbox, four cylinder BN1 of 1953, to the last six cylinder, luxury convertible 3000 Mk III of 1967. An indomitable rally car, a masculine, powerful, almost brutish car, particularly with the competition modifications, which made it deliver its power in a rather heavy-handed way, the Big Healey, as it

Ron Flockhart (Austin-Healey 100S) takes Paddock Bend on the Scottish Charterhall Club circuit, on which Jim Clark and Jackie Stewart raced in the early stages of their careers.

A Mark 1 Sprite at Sebring in 1960, where the make scored class victories in both the 4 Hours and 6 Hours races. The chunky, pert looks of the little cars, and their sensitive handling, made them ideal for young enthusiasts to discover what a well-balanced, lively sports car should feel like.

became known, was to mark the end of an era. It was one of the last of the front-engined, coachbuilt-bodied open two-seaters built in a style which hearked back to the Thirties, but which really reached maturity in the Forties and Fifties.

The inventive genius of the Healey family produced yet another much-loved sports car, the Austin-Healey Sprite. Once again, the recipe was Kimber's, namely the employment of engine, transmission, and running gear from popular models — in this case the Austin A35 and the Morris Minor — and building them into a lively little car which looked and behaved like a sports car. In Mark I form, with bulbous headlights in the bonnet top giving it a pop-eyed frog-like look, the Sprite cost little more than contemporary small saloons. It was economical, it was a car you steered with your wrists; a car which gave its driver a lively ride on its stiff ¼-elliptic rear springs, but which had all the feel and precision of a thorough-bred. The Sprite, and its near-identical derivative the MG Midget, must have taught many a young driver exactly how a perfectly balanced car ought to feel.

Inevitably, as the years passed, the Sprite and Midget became more sophisticated and heavier. They were face-lifted, de-toxed, spongy-bumpered, and bowdlerized until they became unrecognizable. The handling was spoiled and the neat lines ruined before they went out of production in 1979, generally unmourned. The last Austin-Healeys were phased out in 1971, and although MG prepared plans for replacing the Midget, the necessary investment was never made by British Leyland, and the sports car division was closed by 1980.

HRG

Compared with HRGs, Morgans could be regarded as progressive, prolific, and really quite softly sprung. HRGs never altered; only 20 were made in a good year, and most of the vertical movement over bumps was occasioned by the deflection of the tyres.

The cars which Halford, Robins and Godfrey began making in 1935 were already old-fashioned. The beam axle and ¼-elliptic front springs, the engine set well back in the channel-section frame, and the style of Early English Perpendicular about the body were pure Vintage when the first 1½ litre Meadows-engined models made their appearance. In 1938 the engine was changed in favour of a more powerful overhead camshaft Singer, and thus the car remained until production ceased in 1956.

Only two concessions to modernity were ever made: in 1947 an aerodynamic model was introduced, and just before production ended hydraulic brakes were fitted. Like the Morgan Plus Four Plus, the aerodynamic car was not altogether successful, the HRG being constructed with the chassis frame taking its share of the springing,

and its flexure disagreeing with the stiffness necessary to keep a full-width body from cracking and tearing.

HRGs were never fast. The 1500 would do 85 mph, the aerodynamic a little over 90. Their principal virtues were probably a good sense of balance and commendable roadholding of a robust nature. These often enabled HRGs to outperform faster cars in rallies, where the rugged nature of their construction (and the ease with which they could be repaired) earned them many awards, including John Gott's celebrated Coupe des Alpes.

Reflecting again on Morgan, had HRG similarly carried on making their unique Instant Vintage car, they might have kept going almost indefinitely. But in 1955 they announced a new one which not only kept up with the times, but was in many respects ahead of them. The engine was a clever twin overhead camshaft adaptation of the four cylinder Singer, the chassis was tubular with independent suspension all round, and the body was a neat full-width affair.

Events were against the project however. Soon after the Twin Cam was announced in 1955 Singer collapsed, and the engine, which was the cornerstone of the whole design, was discontinued. Triumph and Austin-Healey were already a match for the new car at

less than two-thirds of the price. The project was stopped, and the little firm was forced to turn to other sorts of engineering.

The real problem, however, lay in the economics of producing a car in such small numbers. Three months to make a chassis and two more to erect a body resulted in a truly hand-made car, but it was no way to run a commercial operation, particularly when the market was so restricted and the competition from manufacturers who could invoke economies of scale so strong.

Vintage drivers were supposed to be more interested in engine speed than road speed, so the tachometer, or rev counter, was nearer his line of sight than the speedometer. Oil temperature was shown as well as oil pressure, and under the facia, the handbrake is of the fly-off type for instant release.

Instant antiques. More unchanging even than Morgan, the HRG was postwar, but an earnest enquirer could be forgiven for asking post which war. The mid-Thirties design offered little advance on the mid-Twenties. By the mid-Fifties it was an anachronism in a very proper way, but its days, alas, were numbered.

143

ISO

The Italo-American hybrids tended to be short-lived and frail. Iso never seemed healthy, from the Rivolta of 1962 to the Lele and Fidia which went down with the firm in 1974. They were amongst the early casualties following the Arab-Israeli conflict of 1973.

Yet the conception was superb. A Rivolta would carry four adults in great comfort and commendable quietness at over 100 mph, and would reach 135. The springing was firm, making the ride harsh, especially at low speeds, and the steering was rather low-geared. It needed nearly five turns lock to lock, in order to reduce the effort to the level of American power-steering systems.

It was a large car, weighing a ton and a half, almost evenly distributed between front and rear wheels, which contributed to outstandingly good roadholding. The driver could exploit the strong low-speed torque of the 5.4 litre Chevrolet V-8 by almost ignoring the short, central gearchange. It was possible to accelerate from just above walking pace in top gear if you felt lazy, and still keep up with most traffic, in contrast to the rather more exciting Italian V-12s, which were high-revving and 'peaky', requiring constant shifting to get the best out of them.

By the time of the Iso, leather upholstery and deep pile carpets were more or less obligatory. The stark, lightweight racing shell, with the chassis frames projecting into the passenger space and sometimes a complete absence of door trim, was a thing of the past. Many handsome Mille Miglia-style coupes had ill-fitting doors, Perspex windows, and no sound-deadening at all. The Iso in contrast had wide, rather slippery seats and was quiet enough for the loudest noise at 80 mph to be wind whistle from badly-fitted window vents.

A fuel consumption between 15 and 18 mpg was by no means unreasonable in 1966, but as with so many fine cars, it was to prove the Iso's undoing. The Grifo was a short-chassis two-door, two-seat fastback version of the Rivolta. The lighter weight and the lower body line gave it even better acceleration, and it had a top speed of 160 mph, or even 175 mph with the 7 litre engines which were also available. The Fidia was on a longer wheelbase, with four-door body-work by Ghia, and the Lele was the 1969 2+2 version of the earlier Rivolta.

A short-wheelbase version of the Iso Rivolta, the Iso Grifo was styled by Bertone.

Jensen and Jensen-Healey

An upper-class English quality car of the Thirties, the Jensen was made in a factory at West Bromwich which carried out a large number of automotive projects in its time. After trying out some fairly dreary formal-looking saloons in the early postwar years, Jensen got into the business of building bodies rather in the way Pininfarina and Bertone did in Italy. They not only styled a car, but they laid down a production line to build and trim the finished bodies.

The Austin A40 Sports was one; a two-door open four-seater based on the A40 floor and mechanical units. This provided the capital for Jensen to re-enter the market with a car more in keeping with their rather sportier pre-war output. The 1949 Interceptor was a plain oblong of a car with an oval radiator grille, on an A70 chassis with a 4 litre Sheerline engine.

Jensen competed with the Healeys to build a new sports car for Austin in 1951; the result was that Healey won the design contest, and Jensen got the job of building the bodies for the Austin-Healey 100. This in turn allowed them to develop the Jensen 541, which they introduced in 1953, the world's first production car using glass fibre bodywork.

It was a heavy, rather lugubrious car with a chassis platform made up of welded sheet steel pressings. But it was fast and quiet, like its successor the C-V8, described on its introduction in 1962 as, 'A superb concept carefully disguised as the ugliest car in the world'. The 4 litre six cylinder Austin engine had given way to the 5.9 litre Chrysler V-8, and as the firm's cash flow improved through long-running contracts to trim and paint Volvo P1800 bodies, and assemble Sunbeam Tigers, they developed one of the longest-running and successful of the Anglo-Italo-American hybrids.

The new Jensen Interceptor appeared in 1966, and where the C-V8 was

A front-end restyle identifies the 541S from the 541, which had an oval air intake with a movable shutter to blank it off in cold weather. This 1960 car had a mesh grille with an adjustable internal blind.

Indifferent reliability was chiefly responsible for the short life of the Jensen-Healey, a car built to fill the gap left by Austin-Healey in America. The recipe was right, but something went wrong in the execution, and the car lasted a bare four years.

made at the rate of 160 cars a year, the Vignale-style Interceptor reached over 1200 cars a year. Jensen had become fully-fledged car makers in their own right. But almost as they reached their moment of glory, the picture changed. US Federal regulations suddenly killed both the Austin-Healey 3000 and the Sunbeam Tiger. Jensen found they were virtually on their own. The Interceptor, instead of being the jam, suddenly became the bread and butter; and the award-winning Ferguson Formula, or FF four wheel drive version, although widely acclaimed as revolutionary, was not selling well.

Big, bluff, gutsy, well-made, impeccably finished, a car worthy of attention for its good looks as well as its swift acceleration, the Jensen was a sort of Birmingham Ferrari. It was strong and stylish — a cad's car. And when they brought out the SP, with its multi-choke carburettor which summoned drenching fountains of petrol to provide head-snapping acceleration, you could almost hear the gurgle as the fuel rushed away like the bath-water.

Yom Kippur pulled the plug on Jensen. Sales of the splendid Interceptor slumped. American dealers, bereft of Austin-Healeys, subscribed to the Jensen-Healey, a pretty open two-seater with a Lotus sloper four cylinder engine, de-toxed and lively, but it was to no avail. The car was under-developed and

reliability was suspect. In 1976 Jensen foundered, and an unsympathetic Government, which would later fund Delorean to the tune of £75,000,000 to buy a few votes and a trifling popularity in Northern Ireland, refused a paltry million to save one of Britain's fine cars. Like MG, Jensen employed good craftsmen, honest workers — but not enough of them to create a crisis.

above
The cam covers politely say Jensen, but underneath, the real power is Chrysler. The 86mm stroke V-8 with hydraulic tappets and either Carter or Holley carburettors was an effective reply to lavishly engineered Italian rivals which sometimes offered half the reliability at twice the price.

left
Conceived by Touring of Milan, but officially built by Vignale, the Jensen Interceptor looked every bit a thoroughbred. The opening rear window was the prototype for a number of upper-class hatchbacks.

Jowett

It was a little like a maiden aunt suddenly lifting her skirts and sprinting. Jowett was a plain Yorkshire firm, making staid penny-a-mile flat-twin commercials and lightweight cars, with a virtually one-design policy from 1910 to 1939.

Imagine, therefore, the surprise which greeted the news that they were going in for an export drive and a racing programme. They were making a dishy little fastback that looked like a miniature Lincoln Zephyr with a technical specification to rival a Lancia. It must have made Ben Jowett and his brother Willy of Idle, near Bradford, turn uneasily in their graves.

Their inheritors stuck to some well-tried principles though. The engineering was always good and solid even if the result looked a little racy. The Javelin had a flat four engine and handled so well with its torsion bar springing that it won its class in the Monte Carlo Rally. It then amazed all comers by running in very standard trim in the Spa 24 Hours race — every bit as testing as Le Mans. The little car was encumbered by seats and trim. No lightweight racing shell for the stolid Yorkshiremen who thought everybody else would be sticking to the rules . . .

'Export or die' was the cry, and a sports version of the Javelin was put in hand. Its strong little flat-four was a natural for a small two-seater, and Jowett were determined they should have the best brains to build it. They engaged Dr Eberan von Eberhorst, the former Auto Union designer, to lay out a tubular chassis, on which was mounted quite a surprisingly pretty body, with faired-in headlights and an upright, oval grille.

Von Eberhorst had come straight from Cisitalia, so he applied the most up to date yardsticks to the Jupiter's handling. His principal assistant was Roy Lunn, who was to go to America and mastermind the Mustang I and the GT 40. His technical assistant was David Hodkin of ERA. Jowett did not stint on talent.

When they took one to Le Mans, the only modifications they allowed themselves were those any owner could apply: a special gasket and stronger cylinder head studs to raise the compression to 8.5:1; stronger inner valve springs; high-speed distributor; lightened flywheel and racing plugs. It would still pull in top gear from 10 mph, and do 25 mpg. The cornering was almost free from roll, but the gears were noisy. The Jupiter's only anomaly was a steering column gearshift.

A racing Jupiter was developed; the R1 was a stripped-down open car with exposed wheels, while the R4 had a neat, full-width body of excellent proportions and good wind-cheating shape. It was made in plastic, and its clean lines and sense of style showed that Mr Lunn would soon be too well-known to remain hidden for ever in the Yorkshire Dales.

It was all too good to last. The cars were expensive to make, and once Ford bought the company making the Javelin bodies, the demands for economies of scale became overwhelming. By 1954 it was all over.

Auntie had had her final fling.

Amongst the most remarkable cars in postwar Britain, the Jowett Javelin saloon and the Jupiter sports (*shown here*) were powered by a similar flat-four engine. Their exceptional handling, smart, distinctive styling, and competition record deserved better commercial success.

One of three attempts to revive the pattern of the pre-war Lagonda, the 1961 Rapide was produced on and off for three years, but only 55 were made, and the experiment was not judged a success.

Lagonda

The deep boom of the V-12 still echoed down the memory lanes of Lagonda enthusiasts after the war. Advertised as 'W. O. Bentley's Masterpiece' until Rolls-Royce, who had bought the Bentley name in 1931, objected, the V-12 finished third and fourth at Le Mans in 1939. In fact the V-12 was as much the work of the designer Bentley had brought with him from Rolls-Royce, Stuart Tresilian, but the engine that was to power the postwar Lagonda was indeed Bentley's.

This was a twin overhead camshaft six cylinder, which found itself not in a sports car but in a rather bulgy touring Lagonda which seemed a little uncertain of its role in life.

David Brown made up its mind. When he formed Aston Martin Lagonda Ltd, he phased Lagonda out over the years, but kept the fine engine. He installed it in the tubular-framed Aston Martin, and it became the matchless DB 2.

Lagonda then went into a sort of suspended animation, a name to be brought out and dusted down occasionally when AML made something which was not quite an Aston Martin. There was another V-12 for example, with an ultra-short-stroke 4,487cc engine which proved rather heavy, making the car difficult to handle when it appeared at Le Mans in 1954. It was timed at 148.25 mph on Mulsanne, but the D-Type Jaguar was doing 172.88 the same afternoon on 3.8 litres. The Lagonda crashed into a bank.

In 1961 Lagonda was revived once again, for the Rapide, a sort of four-door Aston Martin DB4 with de Dion rear suspension. It took three years to sell 55 of these unhappy cars with their Edsel-style grille.

Yet Lagonda was not forgotten. As part of the 1976 rescue plan for the firm, it was revived as the label for the Aston Martin Lagonda, the fabulously expensive four-door car with touch-button electronic controls produced ostensibly as the ultimate Grand Tourer.

Ligier

Best-known for Grand Prix racing cars, a small batch of Ligier road cars was built between 1971 and 1976. Guy Ligier, former rugby international and businessman, had raced a Cooper-Maserati in the early years of the 3 litre Formula, setting up in 1969 to manufacture racing cars on his own account.

The Ligier JS2 appeared at the Paris motor show of 1971 and reflected the growing connection with Citroen. The engine was the same V-6 used in the Citroen SM, but instead of being in the front, driving the front wheels, Ligier put it in the middle of the car, driving the rear. Citroen had developed it from Maserati's V-8, so it inherited the unusual (for a V-6) 90° cylinder angle, and employed the five-speed gearbox turned through 180°.

The chassis was a platform of pressed steel panels welded together, the bodywork glass fibre. Once the engine had been enlarged from 2.7 to a full 3 litres, the Ligier was capable of around 150 mph, but only around 100 were ever built. Citroen passed the declining SM assembly on to Ligier, but the firm was more orientated towards racing cars and a full-blown and successful Grand Prix programme.

Marcos

A successful wartime military aircraft was a major source of inspiration for the Marcos. Like the de Havilland Mosquito, it was made with a composite chassis and lower body of marine plywood. The front suspension came from the Triumph Herald, the engine from Ford, and the rear axle from a Standard Ten. It had gull-wing doors and an ungainly-looking plastic body, but the strength and light weight of the 'wooden wonder' helped it to some astonishing successes in British club racing around 1960.

Wood turned out to be a perfectly acceptable material for a lightweight car. Concern over its behaviour in an accident was dispelled following a number of race crashes, when it proved capable of absorbing tremendous impacts, sometimes reducing the hull to matchwood but leaving the driver unscathed.

A more sophisticated version for road use was built by the firm founded by Jem Marsh, who designed the car together with Frank Costin, the aerodynamicist who had worked as a consultant to Vanwall and Lotus. The Marcos GT came with a Volvo 1800 or a Cortina GT engine, the first cars still using bonded wooden boxes as a basis for the chassis.

To reduce height, the 1966 Marcos was one of the first cars to accommodate the occupants in reclining hammock-style seats, borrowing a GT 40 idea. The

Descendant of the so-called wooden wonder, the Marcos GT styled by Denis Adams was revived as a kit car ten years after it went out of production in 1971.

flat, roll-free cornering was a revelation, but luggage space was not large, and its labour-intensive construction never allowed the Marcos to be a cheap car. Close competitors included the Sunbeam Tiger, E-Type Jaguar, and Lotus Elan. The Austin-Healey 3000, which was faster (123 mph against the Marcos's 117 mph) undercut it by a substantial margin, and it never sold in large numbers. Its novelty value persisted, however, and its highly individual lines and exciting handling sustained demand for restored examples long after it had gone out of production.

During the eight years it was produced the Marcos GT altered a great deal. It always looked much the same, but prejudice and those wretched US regulations were against it. The marine plywood parts were never easy to repair, and the technically interesting de Dion rear suspension was abandoned in favour of a well-located live axle. A tubular-framed version was offered with a six cylinder Volvo engine, but production could not be expanded sufficiently for the price to be brought down, and in such a competitive sector of the market, sales were insufficient to support a larger factory and a new model which was poorly received, the extremely plain Mantis.

Matra

Primarily an aerospace firm, Matra usually had partners in their engagements with the motor industry. They established a relationship with Ken Tyrrell, first in Formula 2, then in Formula 1, winning the world championship in 1969 with Jackie Stewart at the wheel of a Matra-Ford in brilliant style.

But the Ford connection had to be broken. Matra had taken up with René Bonnet to build the Djet mid-engined road car, but found the small factory inadequate. Accordingly, they set up a new plant at Romorantin to build a rather more refined car. This was the Matra M530A, shown first at the Geneva motor show in 1967, and the first mid-engined car to sell in anything more than penny numbers.

The engine was a German Ford V-4 which fitted neatly in a new platform of pressed steel built waist-high at the scuttle and around the engine, a real monocoque like the racing Matras. The bodywork was of plastic panels bolted in place, and the concealed headlights were worked not pneumatically, as on the Lotus, but by a strong spring which had its own heavy pedal for the driver to yank them down again. A further curiosity was the gearchange, which

Like the Fiat X1/9, the Talbot Matra Murena made the mid-engined car habitable, with a luggage space in the rear. Unlike the Fiat, the French design made logical use of the available space by seating the occupants three abreast.

because it was designed for a front-wheel-drive car, was the wrong way round when installed in the Matra, with first at the top right of the gate and top bottom left.

The roadholding was good, although the car was underpowered, and some of the obvious problems of the mid-engined layout, noise, for example, or cooling difficulties, were solved quite readily. Matra's Ford connection in racing did not survive the marketing tie-up with Chrysler-Simca in 1969, but the road car did. The 530 went on until 1973 while Matra collaborated in a new mid-engined sports car, the Bagheera.

This was unique in exploiting the width of the car and the absence of a transmission tunnel to make the seating three abreast. A fabricated chassis of tubes and sheet steel provided the basis for the plastic bodied Bagheera, but like the M530A it was never powerful enough, even with a 90 bhp version of the Chrysler Alpine engine to take advantage of its good weight distribution and splendid handling.

It remained in production right up to the PSA takeover of Chrysler-Simca, then it was replaced in 1980 by a new version known as the Talbot Matra Murena.

This took the Bagheera recipe a stage further, with a more up to date body on a steel hull zinc-dip galvanized against rust. The engine was mounted almost over the back axle. A luggage bin at the rear, like the Fiat X1/9, together with the three-abreast seating, made the Murena perhaps the best packaged mid-engined car ever.

Styling mid-engined cars was never an easy task. The Matra M530 was at best controversial. But it did have the advantage of coming to pieces easily. The roof came off Targa-style, and luggage went into the space behind the engine, but mechanical accessibility was always a mid-engined problem. The rear window hinges upwards and a cover on the shelf behind the seats has to be lifted.

Monteverdi

A roll-call of components serves to indicate the relative ease with which a well-financed minor constructor could turn out surrogate Ferraris. Monteverdi had already made a few racing cars before his ambitions took him into the business of road car manufacture. He knew how a fast car should behave, and he had a flair for design which he used, helped by Piero Frua, to build a fastback 2 + 2 round the biggest available Chrysler engine, the 7.2 litre V-8.

The transmission was a Torque-Flite proprietary automatic, although like many of his contemporaries Monteverdi was also to offer a five-speed gearbox made by the German ZF company. The rear axle of the first car was made by Salisbury, the front wishbones and uprights by Alford and Adler, the ventilated disc brakes by Ate, the power steering by ZF and the propellor shaft by Hardy Spicer. Koni suspension units with variable rate coil springs were amongst the off-the-shelf items instantly available to make up the assemblage. Many small firms such as Lotus even used to style their cars round curved windscreens already in quantity production for the likes of the Mark I Ford Capri, so that they would not only be cheap to buy but also could be replaced quickly.

Bumpers, door locks, seats, and all kinds of fittings and furnishings were available from component and accessory manufacturers' stock lists. All the builder was required to do was design a framework to carry them and a shapely body to cover them.

Monteverdi decided on 3mm square tubing, which was welded together, rust-proofed, then sent to Fissore's works in Turin, not one of the fashionable houses, but a builder of special purpose vehicles such as ambulances. Fissore was cheaper because he did not have to support a styling office, but he made up the bodies to Frua's drawings before shipping the cars back to Binningen, just outside Basle, where they were finished.

The character of the Monteverdi was closer to the Bristol or Facel Vega than to the Italo-Americans such as the Iso or the Bizzarini. The emphasis was on finish rather than out-and-out speed, although the effortlessness of the performance proved its strongest suit. Some of the proprietary components turned out better behaved than others of course. Salisbury axles, for example, were not invariably quiet, but they were almost the only ones strong enough to transmit such enormous torque, and the half shafts tended to clunk and groan when the loads were reversed on braking or gearchanging.

Like de Tomaso, Monteverdi supplemented his front-engined cars with a spectacular mid-engined coupe, fully equipped and air conditioned for the American market. He made far fewer of the Hai 450SS than de Tomaso did of the Pantera, however, and it was withdrawn in 1976. Later in the Seventies, the car side of the Monteverdi empire was gradually run down, despite the introduction of the smaller-engined Sierra model.

Peter Monteverdi styled his own cars with a little help from Frua. This is one of his sumptuous 375 models with some rather Ferrari-like overtones, particularly to the rear.

Reliant

Morgan keep cropping up as exemplifying a car which was as unchanging as a car could ever be, yet which never really lost its appeal for long. Reliant on the other hand found themselves diving for gaps in the market, real or imagined, in an effort to sustain sales at an economic level.

In doing so they pioneered some worthy ideas, but by the time real investment was needed for a new model the money was not available, and the make's claim to a place in the market was based on the dubious distinction of being hand-made in an era where many cars were being machine-made rather better.

The Scimitar was the sportiest Reliant, and its major contribution to design was the GTE, or GT Estate style, copied from Volvo who had failed to make very much of it with the P 1800. Reliant allied it to a conventional, rather old-fashioned chassis with a Ford V-6 engine, and the handling, although good by the standards of 1964, when it appeared as the Scimitar coupe, was much less so 15 years later when the firm brought out a convertible in the belief that the Triumph Stag had left them a role to fill.

Strong and well-made, Reliant made a bid to occupy the market left vacant when the Triumph Stag went out of production. But no sooner had they begun making the soft top GTC than customers demanded a hardtop version. This one even has a heated rear window and is fully trimmed on the inside.

Renault

A succession of fairly mundane saloons, many of them rear-engined, with dubious handling, can hardly be considered amongst the sporting classics, but Renault's return to the race tracks produced at least one car which might become a worthy heirloom.

The Renault 5 was a front-drive economy-minded small car introduced in 1972 as a welcome relief from the long succession of rear-engined Renaults. By the late Seventies, their study of turbocharging had convinced Renault that it was the way to go for racing. But it also had a relevance in the economy-conscious days, following the realization that the world's energy resources might be finite, and the sudden quadrupling in the price of oil.

The turbo was able to produce prodigious power from relatively small engines; Renault finally won Le Mans with it in 1978. At once, they announced their intention of taking part in Formula 1, where 1½ litre turbocharged were equated with 3 litre normally-aspirated

engines. Yet it was not simply a matter of extracting maximum power, insisted Renault, turbos used fuel more efficiently.

Their first application to a road car was not, however, to gain economy. In 1980 Renault's competition department built a car whose object was to win rallies, and later in the year they brought out a 'productionized' version which turned out to be one of the most sensational road-going sports cars ever.

Former Grand Prix driver John Miles described the Renault 5 Turbo as an 'Eight-tenths size mid-engined super-car, with acceleration to match, but with the forward visibility of the average saloon, a thoroughbred's steering quality and braking power . . . and so much traction that even without a limited slip differential it is barely possible to spin a rear wheel at full chat out of a slow corner'.

What Renault had done was take an ordinary Renault 5 body shell, cut out the rear seat pan, and put in a 1.4 litre turbocharged engine offering an easy 250 bhp in competition tune. There was a little more to it of course. The floor had

Wide wheels and air intakes on the side give away the mid-engined turbocharged version of the Renault 5. Unsuspecting owners of other Renault 5s may not notice that the rear seat has gone, replaced by a neat cover, turning a modest family car into one of the world's most potent sports cars. An impertinent match for many a thoroughbred with a long pedigree.

above
Renault avoided labelling the Fuego 'sports', but preferred to call it an 'open-plan' car. Smooth body shape was quiet at speed.

In 1957 Amédée Gordini joined Renault to develop performance versions of their standard cars. He had earlier produced some notable sports racing cars, such as this 1953 straight-eight 3 litre. Success at Le Mans eluded him although Gordinis won lesser races.

to be changed, with a new steel sub-frame monocoque within the monocoque, as it were; the suspension was based on the Renault 5 Gordini model at the front, but the rear was necessarily quite unlike any other Renault because it was the only rear-wheel-drive car in the entire range. Wide wheels and tyres were accommodated within bulges in the Renault 5 bodywork, which actually retained quite a large number of ordinary pressings, but in some cases light alloy or grp subtitutes had to be found.

Inside it was properly trimmed and finished, but instead of a rear seat there was a box inside which the engine was quite well silenced.

On almost its first outing the Renault 5 Turbo won the Monte Carlo rally, a tribute not only to the power of the engine, which would propel it at up to 135 mph, but also to the car's controllability on ice and snow, and the fine balance which allowed the driver to apply power while keeping the car pointing in the right direction.

Renault had spent some time earlier toying with the sports car market. They had the 15 and 17 Coupes, based on more ordinary cars, and then the Fuego, a beautifully rounded two-door coupe based on the Renault 18. In the idiom of the Mustang-Capri-Scirocco-Manta, the Fuego was introduced as a larger and less fiery stable-mate.

Sunbeam

The peaks and troughs of a reputation were nowhere better illustrated than by Sunbeam. In the Edwardian years, under Coatalen, it flourished, winning the 1912 Coupe de l'Auto with a resounding 1-2-3. After the war the Italian-inspired twin ohc racer won the 1923 French and Spanish Grands Prix, while a straight-8 won the TT. Sunbeams even took the world land speed record five times between 1922 and 1927.

Within ten years, they had to be rescued by Rootes following the collapse of Sunbeam-Talbot-Darracq. By the late Forties, as Sunbeam-Talbot, they were on the up and up again, with a range of modern-looking coupes based on the pre-war cars. They did well in rallies, and though based on depressingly ordinary Hillman and Humber models, they even took second place on the Monte and won the team prize in the Alpine.

The name Sunbeam alone was applied to a two-seater version of the Sunbeam Talbot 90 which won four Coupes des Alpes in the 1953 Alpine, followed by a Gold Coupe for Stirling Moss and the Coupe des Dames for Sheila van Damm the next year. Appropriately it was known as the Sunbeam Alpine, and even though the engine was

above
Monte Carlo Rally, 1955. Peter Harper in typical Monte weather at the summit of the Col de Valberg in his Sunbeam Mark III, one of the official Rootes entries. The event was won by a Norwegian crew driving a similar car.

left
Distinguished Grand Prix drivers found time to drive in rallies in the Fifties. Stirling Moss and John Cutts drove the Sunbeam Alpine in the Alpine Rally, July 8-14, 1954, seen here before the start at Marseilles. The drive brought them the rare distinction of a Gold Coupe des Alpes by finishing the road section for the third year running without loss of marks.

essentially a pushrod ohv conversion of an old side-valve unit, the well-prepared works cars were able to give a good account of themselves. As the Sunbeam Mk III it even won the Monte Carlo rally in 1955.

The Sunbeam Rapier, which followed the Mark I Alpine and Sunbeam Talbot 90, was too close to the regular Hillman Minx to be a sports car, yet it proved almost as useful a competition car as its predecessor. Nearer the mark was the Alpine Mark II, however much rival Triumph and Austin-Healey owners may have derided its wind-up windows and almost too-pretty styling. It was certainly rather less of a virility symbol than either of its principal competitors, but appearing as it did in 1959, it was perhaps better orientated towards the American market with its Thunderbird look-alike lines.

Yet it never took off in the United States until a 4.2 litre Ford V-8 was shoehorned into the space previously occupied by the four cylinder 1.7 litre. Then it gained a reputation as what was engagingly called, in the jargon of the time, a 'musclecar'. It was never a Cobra, even with the 4.7 litre V-8 and a heavy-duty back axle to look after the enormous torque. But it had acceleration of a very hearty sort, even though maximum speed was never very high, 115-120 mph being quite fast enough for a chassis which started life as Rootes' humblest model, the side-valve utility Hillman Husky.

Once Chrysler took control of Rootes, the employment of a Ford engine quickly became unacceptable. The Alpine/Tiger had never made a great profit in any case, and in 1968 they were unceremoniously dumped. Under the Chrysler regime, the Sunbeam name became simply a badge to be applied when the marketing men wanted a sporting connotation for one of their dreary models. It became steadily devalued until the only Sunbeam left was an economy hatchback made on the rump of the Hillman Avenger by the soon-to-be-abandoned Linwood factory.

A far cry indeed from the glories of the French Grand Prix, and the golden Coupes des Alpes.

The strip along the side was an identification feature which distinguished the Sunbeam Tiger from the four cylinder Alpine. A Ford V-8 gave more life to a car which scored over its contemporaries in style and good finish, as well as the comforts of winding windows instead of detachable sidescreens.

Talbot

By alphabetical coincidence Talbot follows neatly behind Sunbeam; this is the English end with the Coventry-based Competitions Department, inheriting the name that Georges Roesch exalted as invincible in the Thirties, but which was then tacked on to Sunbeam to give it a bit of double-barrelled *cachet* when Rootes perspicaciously bought both.

Faced with the demands of a rally programme required to establish the Talbot marque in the public's eye, 'comps' discovered with some dismay that the range not only had no mid-engined coupe — all the cars were front wheel drive. Except one: the despised Scottish stop-gap Sunbeam.

A programme was put in hand to market a performance version known as the GT, and build a run of 4,500 (to ensure homologation as 'production') of a special Talbot Sunbeam Lotus. With a 16-valve inclined four cylinder Lotus engine, ZF gearbox, and suspension changes, it was thoroughly suitable to inherit the role vacated by Ford when the Escort went over to front wheel drive and became less than ideal for competition.

With 150 bhp in road trim, taut, somewhat nervous suspension, and a weight of only 2,000 lbs, the little Lotus felt exactly like a good-class sports car of twenty years before, as production got under way in 1980. Even with the advantage of modern tyres, road grip remained sometimes elusive in the wet, but it was a car of such delicate balance that the driver kept control even when onlookers might be forgiven for thinking all was lost. On the slippery forest stages of the RAC Rally, Henri Toivonen was able to employ this stunning controllability to beat all comers, breaking Ford's eight-year monopoly.

Modest-looking small hatchback with the speed and power of a real sports car. The Talbot Lotus stormed into the world of motoring sport with a spectacular victory in the RAC Rally.

Bob-tailed Triumph Sports, never officially called the TR1, but precursor of the second-thoughts TR2 nonetheless. Only one of the Walter Belgrove-styled cars was ever made, with the spare wheel exposed at the rear. Standard-Triumph embarked on a sports programme only after Morgan had resisted a take-over bid.

Triumph

The Triumph sports car story is essentially the saga of the series of cars prefixed TR. They altered radically over the years, sometimes with a new engine, sometimes a re-styling or different suspension. By the time they reached the Eighties, they were dart-shaped and forward-looking, but they firmly refused to 'grow up' into mature mid-engined cars with the sort of balance and handling the market demanded. Instead, Triumph liked to preserve just a hint of the Fifties when a sports car liked to be regarded as just a little 'difficult'.

The TR2 was 'difficult'. Developed from the original Triumph TR, shown at the London Motor Show in October 1952 more as a gesture of intent than an avowal of what it would actually be like, the basis was simple. It had a pre-war chassis with cross-bracing, and bodywork carefully designed to be made with the simplest of press-work.

The TR2 was a thorough re-think, with a much stonger chassis than originally envisaged, the Standard Vanguard four cylinder engine brought just within the 2 litre class, and the tail lengthened to get the proportions just right. And all notions of the original car's modest sales prospects of 500 or so were swept away in an avalanche of orders swelled by thoughts of a snappy two-seater which would do 100 mph and

30 mpg. The gearchange was a delight, the hood and sidescreens at least adequate in an age when sports car drivers did not really expect to remain dry, and nobody seemed to care much if the back end hopped a bit on corners or the exhaust boomed. That, surely, was what sports cars were all about.

The chunky looks of the TR2, together with an engine which would perform unflaggingly under great duress, endeared the TR2 to thousands of owners in Britain and North America. The deeply cutaway doors and the firm springing gave a traditional flavour to a design firmly rooted in the Thirties, and which would remain so for many years.

The outline remained more or less untouched until 1961 with the advent of the TR4, which acquired a shapely body by Michelotti. Against the Austin-Healey, the TR was getting distinctly plain, but the new body, with wind-up windows instead of sidescreens, was a big improvement, even though the chassis still owed much to the old Flying Standard. The next major change was in 1965, when the chassis was substantially redesigned to provide independent rear suspension.

Some Triumph enthusiasts claim that this was where the classic TRs stopped. Indeed reactionary American TR fans would have nothing to do with the softer-sprung TR4A, and a special live-axle model had to be made just for them. Soon after the TR4A came the TR5 with six cylinders, sweeping away the

left
Only the second TR2 ever built, this car was used to demonstrate the speed potential of the new model with the cockpit enclosed to reduce drag, and a full-width undershield. Ken Richardson, who was responsible for much of the TR's development, is at the wheel; he took it to the still uncompleted Jabbeke-Ostend motorway in Belgium for an XK Jaguar-style demonstration and achieved 124 mph.

last vestiges of the original TR2, but retaining the feel of a car to which one had to pay attention behind the wheel. It was still a car which had to be driven with a certain amount of feeling; already some perfectly ordinary saloons could out-perform and out-corner it unless the driver was possessed of a high degree of skill with which to make up the deficit.

The 1969 TR6 was a further re-style, this time by Karmann, which cleaned up the front and rear, but left the idiom intact. The TR was still a no-nonsense

open two seater despite the fuel injection (never very satisfactory; the Americans gave it the thumbs down and got their own model again), but the model was clearly an anachronism which would have to go.

The last TR6 was made in July, 1976, by which time the TR7 had been announced, a wedge-shaped two-seat coupe with styling that was at best controversial. It was not even introduced in open form — that would need to wait until 1980, when it could be guaranteed not to affect sales of the dying MGB.

below
Looking somewhat the worse for wear, the winning team of Triumph TR2s in the 1954 Alpine Rally, with Ken Richardson, Maurice Gatsonides and Rob Slotemaker who won a Coupe des Alpes for an unpenalized run, finishing sixth overall, and the Dutch driver T. Kat.

top
Le Mans, 1954, and a
privately entered TR2 took
15th place. The Wadsworth
and Dickson entry was
Dickson's Triumph
dealership demonstration
car, showing on this occasion
the quality of a great car
which could be used in
international competitions
with the minimum of
modification.

middle
Using the new 2.2 litre
engine, the 1958 Triumph
works team scored notable
rally successes, including
gaining fifth place in the
punishing Liège-Rome-
Liège.

bottom
The Group 44 TR6 of
American champion Bob
Tullius, brought to London
following its successful
SCCA season.

162

overleaf
Only the name remained the same. The TR2 of 1953 and the TR7, announced in January 1975, have little else in common. The latest model was very little faster and used more fuel than its simpler ancestor.

First six-cylinder TR, the TR5, one of the shortest-lived of the series with a production life of little over a year. Styling was much the same as the TR4 with some decorative features added.

Not quite the pre-war chassis that tradition has it was simply re-used for the TR series; by the time of the TR4 it had been even more thoroughly modified. The radiator filler is on a long extension to provide for the curved bodywork at the front.

163

The 'miniature E-Type' description applied to the Triumph GT6 is easy to understand in this view showing the neat fastback and the opening tailgate. Interior space was not generous, however.

Whether you consider the classic TR died with the 4A, the 5, or the 7, it was always a car to treasure. No sports car caught the flavour of the days before speed limits or oil embargoes quite like the TR. Cheap and cheerful it may have been, but it had all the machismo of the great sports cars of any age. It was ideal for the up and coming racing driver — Phil Hill raced one in 1955. Early marks were easy to repair, easy to tune, and strong enough for the most testing international rallies. Works teams raced at Le Mans and acquitted themselves well.

The Austin-Healey became more collectable, but the Triumph, however truncated, was the car which survived. Technically, it was never a great car, but it was a very good car indeed.

From 1962, Triumph made the Spitfire, an open two-seater based on the Herald series, with a backbone chassis frame and swing axle independent rear suspension. A competitor to the Austin-Healey Sprite/MG Midget, it never handled as well, nor gained the same reputation for strength and reliability. Its most favoured variants were the six cylinder GT6 coupes, rather claustrophobic but, in the version with properly braced rear suspension, splendid small GT cars.

TVR

Blackpool, where the English went on holiday before they discovered the Costa Brava, was an unlikely place to build a sports car. But the TVR was never quite like other sports cars. As the prolific Graham Robson once put it, 'TVRs were functional rather than refined, and it is a fact that features like sound-deadening, water-sealing, and anti-vibration engineering did not figure prominently in the specification'.

In the same way that Colin Chapman sold his Lotus Elites as kits of parts for home assembly in order to escape the Purchase Tax of the time, so TVRs too were sent out as boxes of bits for the amateur to build in his garage. The customary tubular frame and proprietary engine and transmission were backed up with a plastic body and a list of small parts which included, in the first cars of the mid-Fifties, Volkswagen Beetle suspension for the all-independent springing.

Models proliferated; there was a wide choice of engines, and until the Sixties few TVRs were ever quite identical. Even the Vixens, which appeared from 1967, came with either Cortina GT or MGB engines, and the Tuscan, a development of the Vixen, had a 3 litre V-6 Ford. In between was the US-only Griffith, which followed the vogue for insinuating a large V-8 in the smallest possible chassis, resulting in a crude but highly accelerative car.

TVRs matured under the direction of Martin Lilley, who improved quality and began assembling them on a rather better regulated and disciplined basis at the Blackpool works, now considerably expanded. New models included the M-types and also the Turbo, which might have gained a great deal of prestige for the make if only it had been able to tear up its Lancastrian roots and bring the styling abreast of the times.

This was left instead to the Tasmin, whose pretty plastic body was moulded in halves, like the Lotus, along the waistline. The chassis remained multi-tube, but in a backbone pattern, with fuel injection for the Ford V-6 and the option of automatic transmission. Even a turbocharged model was on offer as TVR joined the ranks of the more regular sports car makers (with all the worries and responsibilities *that* entailed in the Eighties).

Shown at the London motor show for the first time in 1975, the TVR 1600M was powered by a 1,588cc Ford Cortina engine, giving it a top speed around 110 mph.

Vauxhall

Historical connections with Prince Henry and his Trials and the 30/98 apart, Vauxhall did not have much to say in connection with the sporting car. Even then it was only through connections with sport and the necessity, if they wanted to take an active part in competitions, to build at least the minimum number of cars necessary to secure the hallowed homologation.

There were two; the Firenza known as the 'Droopsnoot' on account of the be-spoilered plastic nose-piece, and the 2300 Chevette HS, which provided Vauxhall with their best-ever contender for rally success.

In 1973 Vauxhall embarked on a programme to provide their dealer rally team with a car which would form the basis from which their full-blooded, even more highly modified works rally cars could be developed. The model chosen was a Viva variant, the two-door Firenza coupe, which was provided with a tuned version of the belt-driven ohc 2.3 litre engine giving 130 bhp, and a ZF racing gearbox which could be snapped through any of its five speeds as fast as you could thump the heavy central shift lever. The engineers responsible had remembered that when Lotus set out to make their own engine, they used the Vauxhall sloper four as a starting point, and the 16-valve cylinder head fitted the block more or less exactly.

They were thus able to offer more than 100 extra horse power in their rally car. Even that, however, was not enough, for the Firenza turned out not to be light enough on its feet to beat the Escorts, and after little more than 200 cars the programme was judged not a success and was stopped.

The theme was carried on instead with the 2300 Chevette HS. This had a similar 16-valve cylinder head in a body shell little altered from standard, at least on the outside. The transmission included a five-speed Getrag gearbox and a heavy-duty back axle. Together with suspension changes and wide wheels with extremely grippy tyres, these develoments enabled the little Chevette to outperform many expensive sports and GT cars of even ten years earlier. Using basically off-the-shelf components put together in workmanlike but hardly hand-crafted fashion, capable of withstanding the rigours of off-road rallying, and not displaying any of the temperament or unreliability of extra-vagantly-engineered one-offs of an earlier age, the Chevette represented the sports car wheel turning full circle. It had come back to something between a touring car and a racing car — specially tricked out to compete in rough, tough and gruelling international trials of speed and skill.

The droop-snoot front was grafted on to the regular Vauxhall Firenza body shell in an effort to make a successful rally car. Many useful departures from standard made it an exciting car on the road, but it was never very successful in competition.

Vauxhall's 'homologation special' based on the Chevette, the 2300HS sprouted all the customary aerodynamic features to direct the slipstream where it is wanted.

MINOR CLASSICS

Audi Quattro

If the motor car had not been invented in the closing years of the 19th Century, but in the second half of the 20th, assuming other branches of engineering had progressed as they did, the designers would have come up with something rather like the Audi Quattro. Had there been no roads of course, it would have been the Range Rover, but either way they would almost certainly have chosen to drive all four wheels as the logical corollary of *having* four wheels.

The significance of the Quattro was not so much that it had permanently engaged four wheel drive — there had been cars with this before, notably the Jensen FF. But it had none of the disabling features of previous efforts such as noise, weight, and a heavy fuel consumption. The Audi's power losses were so small that it actually turned out to be more economical, through the second set of wheels being driven and not simply absorbing power.

Starting off with the cross-country Iltis, Audi packed the four-wheel central differential into something the size of a grapefruit, running shafts within shafts to save space. The engine was fuel injected and turbocharged, and although the Quattro, announced at the 1980 Geneva motor show, was primarily meant for competition (it nearly won the Monte Carlo Rally on its first outing) it was an astonishingly tractable and exciting road car. On snow and ice, it was of course in a class of its own, just as the Jensen FF had been, but it did not need the enormous pounding power of a big V-8 to drive it, and since it never wasted anything in useless wheelspin, its acceleration was quite breathtaking.

It was surprising that four wheel drive took so long to reach the sports car world. It never made the grade in Grand Prix racing, partly, many people believed, because drivers tried too hard to make their four-wheel-drive racing cars behave exactly like two-wheel-drive racing cars. They may have failed to exploit the theoretical advantages because they did not want to un-learn their old techniques.

Rather like Auto Union, who took on Bernd Rosemeyer straight from motorcycle racing into their rear-engined Grand Prix car, it may have needed someone with no preconceptions about how a four-wheel-drive car ought to behave.

On the road this did not apply; the advantages were so obvious and real, all that remained to be done to popularize four wheel drive amongst non-sporting motorists was to reduce the complication and expense. After all, there were people who said four wheel brakes were not worth the complication and expense.

Four wheel drive refined. The Audi Quattro was a four-wheel-drive version of the front-drive Audi Coupe which improved on the concept which Jensen had found so unrewarding in the Sixties.

Citroen SM

The application of Citroen technology produced a sports car which was nothing if not memorable. To enjoy it meant accepting a singular blend of space-age engineering with some remarkably pragmatic mechanics by the secondary partners in the SM project, Maserati.

Citroen had, of course, established their reputation for advanced automotive engineering in 1934 with the famous *Traction Avant,* which embodied front wheel drive, monocoque construction, and a host of advanced features. They reinforced this in the mid-Fifties with the DS series, and the remarkable hydro-pneumatic self-levelling suspension which, by the mid-Sixties when they began thinking about a sporting prestige car, had reached a high degree of sophistication.

What they had always been short on was power unit technique. They persisted with old, long-stroke fours which were unworthy of the cars which carried them, and although they had been preparing to embrace Wankel technology, rather more of a match for their advanced chassis engineering, it was taking a long time coming. It never did arrive, but that is another story.

Meanwhile, there was an engine to be supplied for the new car, so an approach was made to Maserati, who

produced a V-6 version of their V-8 in double-quick time by the simple expedient of subtracting two cylinders. The developed version was less straightforward but, as fitted to the Citroen-Maserati, it was left as a 90° engine instead of a 60° like most V-6s.

The car was eventually dubbed the SM, and the startling engineering was matched by an eye-opening body style, a feature of which was a curved glass panel at the front with six headlights, of which four swivelled with the steering, enabling the driver to illuminate the way ahead round corners. The hydraulics not only controlled the self-levelling suspension, they also controlled gearchange, brakes and steering. Yet there was nothing fragile about the SM, and it competed in rallies, helped by 170 bhp which gave it a top speed of 140 mph. A 3 litre fuel injected version was even faster.

Introduced in the heady days of 1970, when the world of the sports car appeared to have an infinite future, within five years the SM had to take its place amongst the gas-guzzling dinosaurs and went out of production. Like so many of its fellows, it was destined to become a classic, preserved in small numbers, for use as a means of recollecting, along with the Flying Scotsman, the Queen Mary, and the Graf Zeppelin, a style of engineering achievement that proved unrepeatable.

An SM pounds the dirt roads in the Morocco Rally.

Daimler SP250

Rushed into production prematurely in an effort to prolong the independence of the ailing Daimler company, the SP 250 might have been more of a commercial success if its creators had taken a little time to design a more appealing body. It was dropped from production following the takeover by Jaguar.

Related to the German firm only by proxy, as the British licensees of the early patents, Daimler had little sporting pedigree. For generations they had been purveyors of limousines and tall, stately cars to the nobility and gentry. Royalty bought Daimlers; it might have appeared *lèse-majesté* to bring out anything so vulgar as a sports car.

Edward Turner had become Managing Director, however, and he had designed motorcycle engines including the great Triumph vertical twin, so in 1959 Daimler did announce a sports car.

It was not at all what people expected.

Certainly the engine was outstanding. It was a V-8 of 2½ litres with a very short stroke, a stiff, five bearing crankshaft, and a single camshaft between the cylinder banks operating inclined valves in hemispherical combustion chambers through push-rods. It was not only a very compact engine but was also very light, being made largely of light alloys. The cylinder head owed something to Turner's splendid motorcycle engines,

and the engine clearly had a great future as the power unit for a new generation of Daimlers.

This was not to be. It was fitted in the SP250, a car unworthy of an engine of such great potential, a hasty lash-up of a TR3A-style chassis with cross-bracing and underslung ½-elliptic springs at the back, and a painfully ugly plastic body. It was 1959, money was getting tight at Daimler, and a new model was desperately needed. The car was fast (121 mph) but the body was poorly finished, the plastic creaked and rattled, doors tended to come open as it flexed, and although later versions improved (they could hardly do anything else) the public did not enjoy acting as development engineers for what was quite an expensive car.

Jaguar took control of the company in 1960, and it was soon apparent that even though the SP250 was no competitor for the E-Type, it was not the sort of car Sir William Lyons wanted to make, and it was dropped. The engine survived in the Daimler 2½ litre V-8 saloon, based on the Mark 2 Jaguar, a successful model which continued in production until October 1969.

Datsun Z

After opening up the North American sports car market with cars like the MG, the big Austin-Healey, the Triumph TR series and various Fiat models, the Europeans, fragmented and individually quite small sports car producers, allowed it to decay. It simply was not worth while meeting US emission and safety regulations for the handful of cars involved.

It was left to Datsun effectively to take over the entire US imported sports car requirement. It eclipsed all makes with one model, beginning in 1969 with the 240Z, a 2.4 litre six cylinder strongly reminiscent of the big Healey in many respects. It had more of the Fiat 124 in its appearance, together with all the driving characteristics Americans enjoyed best — good acceleration, robust handling, reliability, and all the electronic gadgetry they had come to expect.

Stretched and enlarged, it became the 260Z and the 280Z, selling in the

The world's biggest-selling sports car in its various forms, the 240Z Datsun took all the best ingredients of the European sports car, and made them into a car which took America by storm. Plenty of power, good handling, and traditional Japanese reliability resulted in something which was more than a good copy — it established a reputation in its own right as a formidable competition car as well.

large numbers only Japanese manufacturers seemed capable of achieving. Its strength and speed made it a redoubtable rally car, yet it was as a fulfilment of the sports car driver's dreams, especially in North America, that the Datsun Z scored. In a subtle but commercially effective way it took on the *persona* of the Ferrari or the Jaguar which had really created the market in the first place. It began as a surrogate, an imposter, and wound up with a reputation and a tradition of its own — to the extent of aficionados objecting when succeeding models grew fatter and less lithe.

In terms of numbers alone, the Datsun Z must be counted amongst the world's great sports cars.

Delorean

It was not necessarily up to the British Government to evaluate the design of the Delorean. They were more interested in securing jobs for the unfortunate people of West Belfast. If they had, they might have shown a little more concern over some aspects, such as the gull-wing doors, or the engine overhanging the rear wheels, or the sales prospects for a car available in one colour only — brushed stainless steel.

They did not. Instead they subsidized the new factory, for which success depended on a car of dubious worth out-

selling Lotus, Porsche, and all the European sports cars put together. Certainly Lotus engineers did the development work, but only within the design parameters laid down by John Z De Lorean, a former Chief Executive of General Motors. These included the doors, for which there was no structural requirement at all, unlike the 300 SL, on which there was. They also included the Douvrin-built V-6 engine, and the silvery-finished body, designed by Giugiaro.

The Delorean was introduced at the Geneva motor show of 1981, its handling qualities still uncertain, but with doubts abounding over the rearwards weight distribution and the necessity of having different sized tyres front and rear.

Lotus got the job of consulting engineers on the Belfast-built Delorean sports car. The backbone frame resembled that of the Elan series, or the Europa/Esprit, but the engine overhung the rear wheels, unlike the mid-engined design which would have provided more 'European' handling.

Honda S.800

The reputation of the Japanese motor cycle industry was not enough to sustain the high-revving and rather fussy Honda S800 in the sports car market. The engineering was admired, but the customers remained unconvinced.

It was indicative of the concern with which the Japanese were viewed by the European motor industry that when the Honda S800 appeared, like the sun rising over the Eastern horizon, a degree of panic gripped a number of firms. They had seen the camera industry and the motorcycle industry almost squeezed out of existence by the Japanese, and it seemed only a matter of time before the same applied to cars.

Moreover, the one which seemed to threaten the sports car market was made by the firm whose name struck fear into the hearts of motorcycle executives the world over — Honda. Their reputation for efficient, high-revving engines preceded them, and the specification looked stunning. A four cylinder, twin overhead camshaft engine, inclined at 45°, aluminium block and crankcase, and a crankshaft rotating in needle roller main and big-end bearings. True, the engine was only 791cc, but it did produce 70 bhp. It revved to 8,500 rpm, spinning smoothly and quickly up with the sort of metallic zinging noise to which fans of motorcycle 'multis' had already become accustomed.

Well, of course the Japanese *were* going to make their mark on the sports car market, but not in Europe, and not with the little Honda.

It was by no means a light car, and the rather buzzy engine did not appeal

to everybody. The gearbox had to be used a great deal because it was not possible to produce the sort of torque from under 800cc that most sports car drivers wanted or could find readily in Lotus Elans or even Triumph Spitfires. There were a number of ingenious features, such as the step-down gears at the output end of the gearbox, giving a low propellor shaft line under the floor. The front suspension was by torsion bars, and the early models had a novel chain drive, with the chain casings forming trailing arms for the rear suspension. This was abandoned, however, in favour of a conventional live axle, well located with parallel links and a full-width Panhard rod.

Despite its lavish specification the little Honda failed to catch the imagination of the sports car buyers. Perhaps they were too conservative, or the market for a small sports car was simply too crowded with indigenous Austin-Healey Sprites, MG Midgets and Fiat variations. Honda's back-up competition programme got off to a good start in Formula 2, but fell dismally flat in Formula 1, suffering greatly when Jo Schlesser died in the air-cooled Honda during the 1968 French Grand Prix at Rouen.

Lea-Francis

The best days of Lea-Francis were over long before they returned to the sports car market in 1948. This was with a tuned version of the saloon model, with a high-camshaft four cylinder engine designed by Hugh Rose who had designed similar layouts for Riley. The body was a shapely aluminium two-seater with faired-in headlamps and the spare wheel BMW-fashion in the tail.

A separate chassis frame had torsion bar independent suspension at the front; early cars had hydro-mechanical brakes, but these were replaced by fully hydraulic operation. The four-speed gearbox was Armstrong-Siddeley. Production only lasted until 1954. It was a 100 mph car at a time when not many cars were, and it also handled well, but at £1276 it was no match for the XK 120 at just £1263.

There was an attempt to revive the make in 1960 when a car called the Lea-Francis Lynx was built and exhibited at the London motor show. It had a Ford Zephyr six cylinder engine and distinctive styling with a curious circular air intake, but it never got beyond the prototype stage.

The Honda S800 gets taken through its paces.

Mazda RX-7

Dr h.c. Felix Wankel's distrust of an anomaly — making pistons reciprocate in order to achieve a rotary motion — dated back to 1926. His pursuit of a rotary piston engine which would be practical enough to replace the piston-cylinder- crankshaft- camshaft -poppet valve arrangement turned out to be a lifetime's work. It was sponsored by BMW from 1932 to 1936, and by the German aeronautical research institute from 1936 to 1945. Yet they were not primarily interested in Wankel's ultimate goal. They wanted his experience to deal with the problem he was facing in his rotary engine, namely how to make an effective seal between metal surfaces which are banging against one another and getting very hot indeed.

It was 1953 before Wankel felt he had solved the problem. Within ten years his engine was in production, yet within another ten it had been practically abandoned. Hailed as a breakthrough in providing smooth, quiet power, an engine which halved the moving parts, reduced the weight, size, and the expense of making it sounded like some automotive alchemy come true. Licences were bought the world over.

The problem was fuel consumption. The Wankel came on the market just in time to hear the guns of Yom Kippur, and it suffered because at high speed it used a lot of fuel. Engrossed in solving the sealing problem, the developers had neglected the consumption problem.

Plans for Wankel engined cars were shelved. Fortunes in investment in Wankel plant were lost. One company which had turned over practically their entire range to Wankels was Toyo Kogyo, of Hiroshima, such was their faith in it. For a time bankruptcy stared them in the face.

They had to retreat and regroup, but they never lost sight of the Wankel as a technological master-stroke. The logic of the rotary engine remained intact throughout the fuel crises and the huge sums spent in research into improving the engine's consumption.

The perseverance paid off and bore fruit in the creation of a sports car which at the very least was technically novel. Aimed at the Porsche 924 in size and appeal, the RX-7 had turbine-like power,

the little engine spinning easily up to the red line on the tachometer; the dangers of over-revving a Wankel at 7,000 rpm were such that Mazda reinforced the visual display with a buzzer 200 rpm below the limit.

Though its refinement was spoilt a little by extraneous noises, such as intake roar and exhaust resonance, the astonishing absence of mechanical clatter made the RX-7 quite unlike most other sports cars. The fuel consumption problem was never quite solved, although it was alleviated, giving the 106 bhp RX-7 around 18 mpg, below average for the class and a lot worse than a Porsche 924. But it would do 113 mph for owners who regarded technological superiority as a principal attribute of a striking-looking car.

Wankel on the track, the racing Mazda RX7 entered by Tom Walkinshaw found itself classed as a saloon car in the 1981 British championship. It proved the fastest car on the track at a nominal 2.3 litres Wankel equivalency, against 3 litre Capris and 3.5 litre Rovers.

179

Mini

The sporting prowess of the Mini took its creators by surprise. They had set out, led by the inimitable Sir Alec Issigonis, to make a small economy car with plenty of room inside. Issigonis had been obsessed since the Thirties with the idea of a car which made the most of its allotted road space and handled well.

He seized his opportunity by adopting front wheel drive and dropping the engine in sideways, a ploy which was to be repeated in due course not only by other small car designers, but also by most large car designers. The good handling upon which he insisted was not intended to make a sports car out of the Mini, but was there because he believed that even economy drivers should benefit from the knowledge he had gained by building his own Lightweight Special racing car. They would drive more safely in a car which had responsive rack and pinion steering and gripped the road well.

It was inevitable that keen drivers would enjoy the Mini. They enjoy anything capable of out-cornering other cars. It was inevitable too that they would want to apply more power than the standard version offered, and when there is a market demand somebody usually rushes along to fill it. The Cooper Car Company, heavily engaged in Jack Brabham's World Championship-winning Grand Prix cars, contrived with the British Motor Corporation to

make special versions of the Mini to meet this demand.

It was the Mini Cooper that was the last straw for the traditional sports car. The classic open two-seater could just about cope with the indignity of being beaten off the line by larger-engined saloons, but when it came to being quite unable to keep up round the corners, that was too much. There was no longer any point in pretending sports cars needed to be draughty, cramped, noisy or crude. They could have a heater, seat four, remain quiet, and even be refined.

Mini Coopers enlivened touring car races, or production car races as they were called, and emulated the hallowed names of AC, Amilcar, Invicta, Hotchkiss, Renault, Ford, Delahaye, Allard, Lancia, Jaguar, Citroen, Sunbeam, Mercedes-Benz, Panhard and Saab, in duly winning the Monte Carlo Rally, in 1964, 1965 and 1967. It would have been the only car to win it four years in a row but for an undignified and unworthy wrangle in which the French manipulated the regulations to provide somebody else with a victory instead.

But nothing could detract from the achievements of the car which, more than any other, changed the face and the destiny of the sports car. In order to keep up, sports cars had to look to new solutions — to mid-engines, to improvements in suspension and tyres. Other small saloons soon matched the Mini of course, the Volkswagen Golf GTi, the Peugot 104ZS, and many more. But it was a revolution which began with Issigonis's tiny masterpiece.

Front wheel drive and flat, roll-free cornering made the Mini a formidable contender in rallies and races. Victories in successive Monte Carlo Rallies crowned a notable career.

Opel

Like Ford, General Motors in Europe would have rather had nothing to do with sports cars. They interrupted the smooth flow of the production lines and diverted talent which could be better employed doing something more profitable. Until they found competition a useful means of publicizing the product, they remained nervous about cars aimed at the performance market lest they should incur an anti-social image which might put buyers off.

Yet it was publicity of a different sort that was behind the Opel GT. It was conceived as a styling exhibit for the 1965 Frankfurt motor show, as much as anything to demonstrate that GM Europe could do anything that GM America could do, namely style their own two-seater. The lines were based on a number of US dream cars, including some studies for the new Chevrolet Corvette although the floor pan and mechanical units were pure Opel Kadett.

The GT was so well received in Frankfurt, however, that Opel decided to take it seriously. It could never be made in what GM would think of as satisfactory volume, but if the press work could be contracted out, it could be made in commercial numbers, selling through the dealer network. If nothing else, it would be a useful morale-booster for dealers.

The low build and the well-located back axle ensured good handling, and the light weight gave the 1900 version a good turn of speed, with 115 mph available. It was not a large car, and the interior was a bit cramped, but in most respects it was a highly competent European interpretation of the Corvette. It was made in left hand drive versions only, with pop-up headlights and no exterior access to the luggage space. Having opened up the market with the GT, Opel went ahead with the Manta, another coupe based on the Ford Mustang conception of driving the two-door version of a saloon range up-market instead of down. The saloon was the Opel Ascona and it took up more or less where the GT left off in 1973.

Roomier, and less of an out-and-out sports car, the Manta, like all Seventies' Opels, had a Vauxhall equivalent, the Cavalier Coupe and subsequently the Sports Hatch, but it was not a competitions front runner until 1981, when a '400' version was announced. This was based on the Ascona 400 (the figure was the number which had to be made to secure homologation in the appropriate production car category), with improved location for the coil sprung back axle, and a fuel injected sixteen-valve cylinder head.

Like the Asconas, the Manta 400 was a high-performance road car on which the competition department could base an even faster rally car.

Dream turns to reality; the Opel GT was one stylist's concept car which turned out to have a practical application.

182

Riley

Rileys began as touring cars soon after the turn of the century, and effectively ended as touring cars some 57 years later. In between were some famous sports cars, such as the Riley Nine of 1926, the first to feature the enduring engine, with two camshafts high on each side of the cylinder block operating the valves through short pushrods. This layout gave a hemispherical combustion chamber and inclined valves — all the best ingredients for efficiency and power — whilst avoiding the worst complications of an overhead cam layout. The Nine was a four cylinder of 1,087cc, and the principle was adhered to in engines of up to 2½ litres.

Rileys were never wildly expensive sports cars; they cost more than MGs but not as much as Bentleys or Aston Martins. Following the war they remained firmly middle class but reverted to a less sporting role. The Thirties, while providing Riley with a formidable reputation in racing, brought the firm to the verge of collapse, and it was swallowed up by the Nuffield organization. It did not lose its identity at once, however, but was given over to four-seat saloons of sporting inclination, with precise steering and a good turn of speed.

The 1½ and 2½ litre RM saloons of the Forties were handsome cars and even though basically pre-war designs featured torsion bar independent front suspension, rack and pinion steering, and a crisp, remote-control central gear lever when an ephemeral fad was providing many contemporaries with the abhorrent steering column shift. The 2½ litre, at a time when sports cars were notably absent from the catalogues (there was no need for them, manufacturers could sell as many ordinary cars as they could get the materials for) could do 100 mph and handled like a sports car.

A three-seat roadster version was offered for a time, and an open four-seater, but not many were made. Production of the RMB 2½ litre ceased in 1953, when it was replaced by the Pathfinder; the RME 1½ litre carried on until 1955.

Introduced in March, 1948, on the 9ft 11in 2½ litre chassis, the three-abreast-seater Riley Roadster was for export only at first. A four-seat drophead coupe followed later in the year. The long-tailed roadster suffered from that mercifully passing fad, a steering column gearchange.

Saab

If nothing else did, the competition record of Saabs would have distinguished them as sports cars. The rally victories of Eric Carlsson driving the three cylinder two-stroke, then the V-4 engined saloons, with their rounded, teardrop styling, became legendary. The high ground clearance, stong construction, and good handling of the front-wheel-drive Saabs won them the RAC Rally three years running (1960, 1961 and 1962) and the Monte twice (1962 and 1963).

Saabs enjoyed the reputation of sports cars outside Sweden, largely as a result of Carlsson's exploits, but in 1966 the firm embarked on a sports car proper, the Sonett. They had made prototypes before, but the Sonett was the first to reach production, at first with the old three-cylinder two-stroke engine, but by 1968 with the German-built Ford V-4.

Sonetts were never made in large numbers, assembly being in the hands of an outside contractor to whom Saab supplied the floor pressings, suspension and engine-transmission units. The plastic body was altered for the Sonett III in 1970; other changes were a larger (1½ litre to 1.7 litre) version of the V-4 engine giving a top speed of better than 100 mph. Heavily dependent on US sales, the Sonett suffered from increasingly stringent emission laws, and by 1974 it had been withdrawn.

Saab scored notable success as a pioneer of turbocharging with the 99 and 900 series of saloons. Strong, front wheel drive, and fast, they never attained the competitive heights of their predecessors; Saab nevertheless kept their sporting reputation long after they lost their sports car.

Saab Sonett Mk II, 1966.

Volvo P 1800

Like so many Volvos, the P1800 turned out rather heavy to give a thoroughly sporting performance.

The conditions of the northern winter, the dirt roads, and a keen competitive spirit amongst drivers have all been held responsible for a strong demand on the Scandinavian market for cars which handle well. Just as French cars often tended to have a smooth ride on pavé, so Swedish cars were required to behave predictably on snow and ice.

When Volvos were exported, it was often in a sporting role, even though the firm made few real sports cars. Like the Saab Sonett however, Volvo entrusted the assembly of the 1800 sports car to others, until their customary concern over quality made them bring it under more direct control.

Once again, like Saab, the engine and transmission, and the suspension of the 122 saloon formed the basis, not for a plastic-bodied car, but for a rather high-waisted two-door coupe made by Pressed Steel and finished by Jensen.

Known as the P1800 when it was introduced in 1960, and the 1800E when production was taken to Sweden in 1964 and the engine fuel injected to give it a little more life, it was subsequently restyled to a configuration successfully copied by Lancia and Reliant. This was the sporting estate car known as the P1800ES which did well over 110 mph (a little noisily however — body drumming was a problem) until it was withdrawn in 1974.

Index